The Wisdom of the
BEGUINES

—————— *The Wisdom of the* ——————
BEGUINES

The Forgotten Story of a Medieval Women's Movement

LAURA SWAN

BlueBridge

Published by
BlueBridge
An imprint of
United Tribes Media Inc.
Goldens Bridge, New York

www.bluebridgebooks.com

Originally published in hardcover in 2014 (ISBN 9781933346977).
First published in paperback in 2016 (ISBN 9781629190082).

Library of Congress Control Number: 2014948523

Cover design by Cynthia Dunne
Cover art: Rogier (Roger) van der Weyden (c. 1399–1464), Portrait of a Woman with
a White Headdress, c. 1435. Photo Credit: bpk, Berlin / Gemaeldegalerie, Staatliche
Museen, Berlin, Germany / Joerg P. Anders / Art Resource, NY
Text design by Cynthia Dunne

Printed in the United States of America

20 19 18 17 16 15 14 13 12 11

CONTENTS

INTRODUCTION

THE CITY OF BRUGGE (Bruges) in Belgium has a charming medieval core including a network of canals and waterways. Hidden among the carved stone buildings and emerald waterways is a quaint walled village with the name *Begijnhof ten Wijngaard* (Beguine Community of the Vineyard)—a beguinage, founded around 1242. When I visited Brugge some years ago, our tour guide told us that the medieval women who had inhabited this village, known as beguines, were "pious old ladies praying and doing good works until they died." Something grated within me. I intuitively knew this description was incorrect. I was drawn to this village of beguines inside the city and wished that one day I would learn the truth concerning their lives and ministries.

The beguines began to form in various parts of Europe over eight hundred years ago—around the year 1200. Beguines were laywomen, not nuns, and thus did not take solemn vows and did not live in monasteries. The beguines were a phenomenal way of life that swept across Europe, yet they were never a religious order or a formalized movement. And they did not have one specific founder or rule to live by. But there were common elements that rendered these women distinctive and familiar, including their common way of life, chastity and simplicity, their unusual business acumen, and their commitment to God and to the poor and marginalized. These women were essentially self-defined, in opposition to the many attempts to control and define them. They lived by themselves or together in so-called beguinages, which could be single houses for as few as a handful of beguines or, as in Brugge, walled-in rows of houses enclosing a central court with a chapel where over a thousand beguines might live—a village of women within a medieval town or city. And each region of Europe has its own beguine stories to tell.

Some beguines were suspected of heresy, and often politics were the driving force behind such charges. Certain clerics defended beguines against charges of heresy, while other women had to go undercover by joining a Benedictine or Cistercian monastery. Beguines had male counterparts called begherds— but the begherds quickly morphed into formal religious orders such as the Alexian Brothers.

Beguines existed all the way into the twenty-first century— news agencies reported the death of the "last beguine," Marcella Pattyn, in 2013. She was in her early nineties and had lived in Belgium. However, there are reports of young women making spiritual promises and seeking a beguine lifestyle, both in Europe and North America. Some of these new beguines live with their parents, or by themselves, and others have created informal communities.

In more recent travels I have had the opportunity to return to Brugge and also to visit the beguinages in Ghent, Leuven

(Louvain), and Diest (all in Belgium), as well as the beguinage in Amsterdam. Scholars have identified 111 medieval beguinages in Belgium alone, and thirteen of them are UNESCO World Heritage sites: Ghent, Leuven, Diest, and Brugge; Hoogstraten, Lier (Lierre), Mechelen (Malines), and Turnhout; Sint-Truiden (Saint-Trond), Tongeren (Tongres), Dendermonde (Termonde), Sint-Amandsberg (Mont-Saint-Amand-lez-Gand), and Kortrijk (Courtrai). Today most homes within the surviving beguinages in the Low Countries are affordable housing for the elderly, writers, or artists. The exteriors and gardens are kept as they might have been when beguines—the original builders—lived there. Most of these beguinages will have one home, furnished appropriately for the medieval period, open for visitors to explore and learn about the beguines and their way of life.

When a spiritual genius inspired (and sometimes formed) a new religious movement—as with Teresa of Ávila (1515–1582) and the Carmelites or Jeanne-Françoise de Chantal (1572–1641) and the Visitation nuns—extensive testimony and documentation had been saved. All this material became part of official records that historians can access. But because the beguines were never a formal movement, no medieval or early modern archivist or historian was ever tasked with documenting their lives and teachings. Who were these women? What did they do to earn a living? What was their inner life like? How did their communities function?

Around 1980, scholars began to take a real interest in the beguines as an independent women's movement, and they have been unearthing evidence of beguine life and values, going in search of historic facts. They are scrutinizing old archival records in Europe—land sales, land deeds, legal documents, contracts, rent books, financial accounts, obituaries, wills, and court records—in order to discover what the beguines were actually doing. Wills reveal what beguines possessed and the care with which they considered the disposition of their property. In Douai (northern France), for example, municipal archives contain around two thousand wills related to the beguines and their dispersal of property (both to individual beguines and to beguinages), dating from the thirteenth to the sixteenth centuries.

The writings of a few beguines have survived the centuries, mostly because monastic women kept copies of the texts safe in monastery libraries, and they are now being located, are undergoing new translations and analyses: what is the authentic voice of each woman—and what is the voice of her secretary, chaplain, or biographer (who might have had his own political agenda)? Beguine writings include dictated visions, poetry and prayers, some correspondence, as well as *vitae* (singular *vita*). These are biographies but not in the modern sense—the goal of a vita is to tell a good story, much like a morality play, while demonstrating the sanctity of the vita's subject.

Scholars remind us that the vitae were composed with "attitude," meaning the writer (who was often not the beguine featured) shaped the story in order to highlight and promote sanctity, to emphasize a moral story or argument, and to convert people to a better life. Ensuring exact historical details was never the intent of these texts. But why were some vitae more popular than others, and why did some vitae remain local while others were disseminated throughout Europe and in numerous languages? Experts have been analyzing the vitae in an attempt to unearth valuable neglected history, to gain insight into the cultural contexts that produced them, and to discover the mindset and aspirations of laywomen.

The narratives by beguines that have survived were usually recorded by their confessors and refined until the women were satisfied with the construct. These are stories of a woman's search for a genuine self, seeking to put into language the process of discovering that self, and inviting others to join her in that search. Beguines lived in a medieval world governed by men and according to values that validated masculine experience. The mere search for a self by a woman was perceived as undermining "male privilege," even though that was probably not her intent.

Beguine writings—which have survived wars, pestilence, book burnings, and the vagaries of life—also reveal something of their everyday life: we have snippets of commentaries, especially on the Bible, written or dictated by beguines; sermons created by these women as well as favorite sermons by others that they saved and shared among their friends; and martyrologies (lists of martyrs and saints to be venerated) from beguinages that reveal saints for whom beguines held a particular devotion, and therefore express the values the women themselves treasured.

Psalters (books of hours) owned by beguines were often crafted at their direction, meaning they dictated which texts and illustrations were to be included. Frequently these books contained beguine poems and prayers not in common use by the church. The biblical books that beguines owned were also crafted at their direction and the illuminations reveal much about their spiritual world.

Scholars today also study medieval sermons, extracting stories of beguines and comparing them to other sermons. These extracted stories are called *exempla* or parables, and their original selection was meaningful: people share the stories that catch their curiosity or challenge their thinking; they do not pass on stories that fail to touch their hearts. In addition, liturgists and musicologists are reviewing medieval music and liturgy compositions, noting the context from which they emerged and identifying music composed or commissioned by beguines. This music includes sacred hymns and chants as well as recreational secular songs.

Art historians have been studying the relationship between sculptured artwork of the late medieval period commissioned or created by beguines in northern Europe and their spirituality. Beguines favored *pietàs*, representations of the Virgin Mary grieving the crucified Christ, usually held in her lap; sculptures of *Virgin and Child*; and the *Christuskindje*, or Christ-child, Jesus portrayed as an infant. A particular artistic style emerged which some historians attribute to the specific requests of beguines who had commissioned these artworks. As with our texts, the art we create and preserve can tell a fascinating story.

Even medieval records of alleged heresy open a window into the lives of the beguines for us. Accusations of heresy against beguines resulted in official church investigations called visitations. A team of men, usually chosen by the local bishop, was sent to a beguinage to ascertain whether any evidence existed to support charges of heresy or immoral lifestyle. The resulting documentation, correspondence, and visitation reports reveal much about the quality of life and devotional practices of the beguines. The lives and any possible writings of beguines who had in fact been declared heretics are also being reexamined, to find out if a woman's teachings were truly heretical—or if her condemnation was politically or financially motivated.

Consequently, our understanding of the influence beguines had within the church is being revamped. Their ministry impacted education and health care, their intellectual pursuits influenced the theology and lifestyles of preachers, and certain orders of Catholic sisters had their foundation in beguine communities.

Clearly, more research is needed. Archaeologists, anthropologists, and anthropological architects need to uncover beguinages buried in the mesh of buildings, particularly in Italy and Spain. This work might tell us more about how beguines lived and ministered in specific parts of Europe and especially how they maintained some sense of independence in a society that forever attempted to control them. Scholars of Eastern European cultures and of Spanish culture, for instance, have just begun to scratch the surface of the legacy of beguines and comparable laywomen in their respective regions. The women had been there, but they had been embedded in someone else's story.

My childhood in the 1960s was spent in a well-educated and religiously diverse neighborhood east of Seattle. I was taught by the Sisters of St. Joseph of Peace, who had reinforced my parents' values of respecting the elderly, the importance of neighbors and community, and the concern for social justice. I observed my mother and her friends debating politics and social issues within the context of their faith traditions.

My great-aunt Mary Consuela, a feisty Sister of Mercy, passionately served the poor and worked in the civil rights movement in the Deep South. I could never quite relate to a passive and distant Blessed Virgin Mary who looked down benevolently from heaven, seemingly unconcerned with human suffering. A docile Mother of God on the one hand and my great-aunt, who embodied a fierce compassion for the vulnerable, on the other, created quite the contradiction for me.

In my first round of graduate school I began encountering the writings of medieval women—Angela of Foligno, Catherine of Siena, Catherine of Genoa, and others. These women were mystics and reformers, poets and preachers, servants of the poor, founders of movements, and leaders in their own right—women much like my great-aunt, women who gave voice to their own experience of the Divine, women with whom I could relate. In recent years I have come to discover that many of these medieval women were in fact known as beguines.

I joined the Benedictines in the midst of rapidly declining numbers of sisters. We vowed religious are passionate about our way of life and are committed to the mission of our diverse communities. We look to the past to inform our present as we discern the direction of our future. There have been seasons in history when the number of vowed religious dropped precariously, sometimes because of disease or war, sometimes due to social upheaval, and sometimes due to outright persecution. We are in the midst of enormous paradigm shifts. Some individual monastic communities will need to be closed. We know religious life will look different in the future. Large numbers of laywomen and laymen are already connected to monastic communities as affiliates, oblates, tertiaries, and there are new expressions of monasticism. Many young people are seeking creative ways to live lives of simplicity and justice, contemplative prayer and service to others.

I am intrigued that many beguine communities survived for a long time despite oppression, wars, the plague, and other human and natural disasters. Beguines lived through—and helped propel—times of great transition and reform. What strength of spirit protected the lives of these women and their beguinages? What can we learn from them? What might they teach us?

It is problematic to project modern concepts and ideologies on historical figures. Yet with near perfect pitch, medieval beguines are echoing my aspirations for contemporary society. The medieval world was in some ways not so different from our own: rampant greed, political strife, endless war, environmental devastation, the outbreak of pestilence, religious upheaval and killing in the name of God. Beguines courageously spoke to power and corruption, never despairing of God's compassion for humanity. They used their business acumen to establish and support ministries that offered education, health care, and other social services to the vulnerable. And they preached and taught of a loving God who desired a relationship with each individual person while they criticized those who used God's name for personal gain.

I am convinced that the beguines have much to say to our world today. They invite us to listen to their voices, to seek out their wisdom, to discover them anew.

I

WHO WERE THE
BEGUINES?

OMEN WHO WERE called "beguines" were from every social class—aristocrats and patricians, merchants and guild members, widows or daughters of knights, the urban poor as well as rural poor. And beguines could be of almost any age—from around fourteen years old up to their eighties and possibly beyond. Self-supporting and single or widowed, these women stood out for their spiritual and personal independence, preaching in public and debating with select theologians and biblical scholars. Many beguines lived in private houses, home to just a few of them. Some spent part of their lives as hermits or recluses yet maintained some contact with their families, spiritual seekers, and other beguines. Many lived alone while meeting daily with fellow beguines in a favorite chapel or church for the celebration of mass, the Divine Office, and other gatherings for prayer.

Beguines encouraged fellow laypeople to follow their example and take responsibility for their own spiritual education. Beguines were passionate about ministry. They were astute in business, active in the emerging money economy, and committed to serving the less fortunate in various ways. These "gray women"—so named for their preferred attire of gray homespun wool with hooded capes—were given the nickname "beguine" in the Low Countries (from the root *begg-*, meaning, to mumble or to speak unclearly),[1] which was originally meant as a mocking term, suggesting these women were hypocritical or deceitfully pious. Powerful medieval men were insulted by the presence of women living independent lifestyles and thus publicly derided them. How absurd were these women to think that they could live without the guidance of a father or husband or cleric? How could women be trusted with their own spiritual journey? Even teach and preach and handle their own money? Yet for many people the term "beguine" soon became a compliment because these women had earned the respect and support of their fellow citizens, and even that of some political and religious leaders.

While beguines were known throughout Europe, each region had its own colloquial name(s) for them. In northern France such lay religious women were called *fins amans* (true lovers) or *béguines*, and in regions of Spain *beatas* (Latin for "blessing"). In parts of Italy they were called *penitentiae* but also *pinzochere* (meaning, devotee) and *bizzoche* (meaning, penitent), and in Lombardy the *humiliati* (meaning, the humble or poor). In Germany they were the *beg(h)inen*, in Sweden the *beggina*, and in Denmark the *beginer*. All these names—and there were various others—reflected local usage for the same reality: an informal movement of independent women who defined for themselves what it meant to live according to gospel values. (In medieval Britain, people were aware of the beguines and their lifestyle, but the movement never really took root there.)

There was no single founder, no specific constitutions, no formalized lifestyle for beguines, yet this movement of extraordinary diversity had a significant impact on society and the church for centuries. Women began stepping outside the strictures and confines inflicted upon them by the church and the prevailing culture, seeking to express their faith as they felt called to it. They sought out preachers of their own choosing, secured informal copies of the Bible that existed in the vernacular and learned its texts, and began experimenting with ways of literally imitating the lives of the first apostles. Frequently, beguines gathered around a gifted female master teacher called a *magistra* (someone recognized as a master of theology) who was renowned for her eloquence and spiritual authority. Beguines forcefully embraced the call to holiness as *every* person's journey and not just that of professional "holy people," namely priests, monks, nuns, and others in formal religious life.

Beguines were *not* nuns. Nuns lived in monasteries—in medieval times, the terms "abbey," "monastery," and "priory" were used for both monks and nuns—and most nuns at the time followed the ancient Rule of Benedict. They rarely left their monastery grounds and were under the authority of their abbess who was in turn under the strict control of the local bishop. Nuns made solemn profession—stability, obedience, and conversion of life—before the local bishop, vows that were legally binding and recognized by the authorities in Rome. Solemn profession also meant that a woman was renouncing her right to claim any family inheritance. (While celibacy was not an outspoken part of solemn profession, it was always understood to be an essential part of the monastic life.)

Throughout Europe, beguines followed no formal rule of life such as the Rule of Benedict, and the local bishop exercised no more authority over beguines than he did over any other layperson in his diocese. Because beguines paid taxes on their property and income, and their tax revenue was needed by the local government, they enjoyed a certain degree of protection from the church. They were self-supporting—possibly as artisans, in commerce, or through their investments—and they were very protective of their personal and collective freedom, both in their own lives and in their service to the destitute. For the most part, beguines were free to make their own life choices and to move about their town or city as they wished (as long as they had a companion with them), and women of every family status would become beguines: they were unmarried or widowed, or they would leave their husbands,[2] or raise children alongside. And they could at any time cease being beguines and get married.

Traditionally, most monasteries for nuns were located in the countryside and not in cities. Nuns were granted religious exemption from paying taxes on their property and income, and they had to be self-supporting. But because they were not permitted to work outside the clearly defined boundaries of the monastery, they needed to have a dowry that could contribute to the support of the monastic community—hence most nuns came from wealthy families. Because of their cloistered way of life, nuns had limited contact with their families, and upon entering the monastery, friendships were essentially severed. They enjoyed very little opportunity for ministry—it was usually limited to educating select daughters of the elite, or their ministry might have been prayer (which was deeply valued in medieval times), writing, copying manuscripts, composing music, or creating artwork.

Beguines, on the other hand, lived and ministered primarily in the growing urban areas of Europe (the principal exception were beguines who worked with lepers, since lepers were not permitted in cities). Beguines worked and prayed and socialized together but also maintained close contact with family, friends, and neighbors. While some lived with their parents, many beguines used their sources of income to purchase homes near the chapel or parish church where they gathered together for prayer. These homes became known as "convents" (which is the origin of the modern term), and they were shared by two to four—or, in larger homes, up to twelve—beguines. They usually purchased homes near each other, slowly taking over neighborhoods. Sometimes these grew into larger complexes that became known in the Low Countries as court beguinages, because of a large beguinage's central courtyard that all beguines living there shared. Such courtyards functioned much like medieval village greens (they were not cloisters as existed in monasteries), and outer walls and gates provided the beguines with privacy and security. Other court beguinages began as significant complexes on the edge of a city or large town, where a spacious tract of land was provided and the beguines began construction. (In the pages to follow, the term "court beguinage" refers specifically to these larger complexes, while "convent" refers to single dwellings of usually a few beguines. The term "beguinage," on the other hand, is used for various beguine dwellings.)

Women's monasteries tended to last for generations unless obliterated by war, reformation, or revolution. Beguine convents were more fluid—often within a generation or so a group of beguines living in one location had died off and their home was sold. Other beguinages managed to stay put through multiple generations, which usually meant that aunts had passed homes on to nieces, allowing close family ties to keep the beguinage intact.

Nuns were steady supporters of the beguines. Frequently women's monasteries loaned land to groups of beguines on which they could establish their informal communities, and sometimes monasteries also assisted with construction costs. Nuns were also great defenders of the beguines against charges of lewdness or heresy. Women's monasteries oftentimes copied texts written by beguines, thus preserving these writings over the centuries.

When women first chose to become beguines across Europe around the year 1200, it was as individuals or small groups; as business women, itinerant preachers, or hermits; and usually associated with a local chapel or parish church. They emerged in the midst of a so-called first renaissance when European society was transforming itself from a narrowly defined structure of a great many peasants (who were mostly poor and uneducated) ruled by a small elite of aristocrats and church leaders into a broader society with a growing merchant class and a more sophisticated political system. Several factors propelled this renaissance and supported the emergence of the beguines, including the Crusades and courtly culture, emerging cities and their fledging universities, a new money-based economy, the growth of lay spirituality and the cult of the Virgin Mary, as well as new monastic orders.

As men in western Europe began to depart their villages and towns to join the First Crusade (1096–1099), women had to handle much of the work traditionally fulfilled by men, such as farming and blacksmithing, and they came to enjoy their newfound independence. Many men never returned from the Crusades, thus leaving women permanently responsible for their families. Increasingly, women attempted to leave the countryside and its villages, moving to the major economic centers—the growing cities. The shift from a farming and barter economy to a coin-based economy (which allowed for an increase of trade and the expansion of trade routes) resulted in the rise of a merchant class, the medieval bourgeoisie. More people of both sexes enjoyed access to money. Women flocked to the cities, especially in the Low Countries, Germany, and northern Italy, to seek employment and independence. Textile industries were flourishing with the growth of trade, and women proved themselves adept in these industries. Many of these female workers became beguines.

People in Europe had awaited the arrival of the new millennium both with fear and hope—they expected Jesus Christ to return. But when the year 1000 passed without seismic shifts, a common belief emerged that Jesus had not returned due to the sinfulness of people and of the church, and thus a call for reforms developed. At the same time, a new awareness emerged that *all* people were called to holiness and could enjoy an immediate consciousness of God's presence. Flight from the world was no longer a perceived requirement for attaining divine grace. God could be found in the secular realm and in the midst of ordinary everyday life.

The new millennium also saw a great boom in the building of new churches, and people were much drawn to these new houses of God. An era of reform within the church, known as the Gregorian Reform (named for Pope Gregory VII, who reigned from 1073 to 1085), brought new life to the church from within.

As laymen and laywomen across Europe began to take their faith into their own hands, they also continued to demand reform within the church. Emerging from this discontent was a phenomenon (it was *not* a formal movement) called the *vita apostolica*, which means the "apostolic life" or "the life of an apostle." Beguines were a powerful expression of the vita apostolica.

Both medieval laypeople and monastics were holding in the highest esteem the first followers of Jesus—particularly the early church in Jerusalem—as having lived the ideal Christian life.

The author of the Acts of the Apostles had described the earliest believers (Acts 2:42–47), who were known as Followers of the Way, as gathering frequently to hear the apostles teach while also keeping up their daily attendance at the temple. Followers of the Way shared in a common life, meeting regularly for meals, prayer, and ministry, and selling their property and possessions to meet the needs of the poor. The author of Acts reported an atmosphere of anticipation, awe, and unaffected joy among believers of Jesus Christ. Essential to Followers of the Way was to live by the Christian baptismal creed, "There is no such thing as Jew and Greek, slave and free, male and female; for you are all one person in Christ Jesus."[3]

The medieval men and women who embraced the vita apostolica were intent on imitating this early Christian lifestyle as literally as possible, and most adherents of the vita apostolica were recognized by leading lives of profound simplicity, generosity to the poor, taking care of lepers, and daily attendance at prayer in a church. Beguines and other laypeople asked themselves: How did Jesus want us to live? How did early followers of Jesus behave? Why does our own church not look like the church of the early apostles—why is corruption tolerated? Beguines were especially adept at imitating the first apostles and exhorting others to do likewise (and therefore they were becoming a threat to some of the men in power).

The essential foundation of the vita apostolica was voluntary poverty—a literal interpretation of the poverty of Christ. Medieval followers of the vita apostolica sought to make Christ present on earth and to restore the church to its original, primitive expression. At the same time, these women and men were reacting with growing alarm and disdain to the new market economy based on coinage and money-lending with interest charged. Followers demanded of themselves acts of austerity and works of charity with the intent of protecting themselves from vanity and undue dependence on material goods. Among the adherents of the vita apostolica were the newly emerging mendicant orders—the Dominicans and Franciscans—which had both begun in the early thirteenth century. Mendicants took religious vows and freely moved around Europe to preach and teach in universities, churches, and public squares; they did not have the same attachment to a specific monastery as the monks and nuns. In principle, mendicants lived off alms and thus were referred to as wandering beggars.

Beguines distinguished themselves from other followers of the vita apostolica in their comfort with the new market economy—in fact, their freedom depended on it. Some vocal leaders of the vita apostolica demanded that followers seek absolute privation even if this privation limited the ability to aid those unable to care for themselves. But beguines disagreed, and they used their keen business sense to earn the money needed to help the poor. Beguines pooled their resources in order to serve the sick and destitute by building and operating infirmaries and almshouses.

Alongside the vita apostolica arose fresh expressions of monasticism as well, including the new orders known as Cistercians, Carthusians, and Premonstratensians in the late eleventh and early twelfth centuries. Monastics such as Anselm of Canterbury (c. 1033–1109), Robert of Arbrissel (c. 1045–1116), Bernard of Clairvaux (1090–1153), Hildegard of Bingen (1098–1179), Héloïse (c. 1101–c. 1164), Marguerite d'Oingt (c. 1240–1310), and Gertrude of Helfta (1256–c. 1301) exemplified the creative genius in the monasteries. The monastic world was calling itself back to this gospel vision, to the original intentions of Saint Benedict, and to a deeper observance of the contemplative life.

The cult of the Virgin Mary, a deep devotion to the mother of Jesus, also came to life with the new millennium. While Mary had always been honored, now artwork, music, and piety expressed a fresh and strong relationship with her. Stained-glass windows, sculptures, and frescoes supported and expressed the growing importance of the Madonna in the lives of ordinary believers.

In the early thirteenth century, the sisters Countess Joan (1194–1244) and Countess Margaret (1202–1280) of Flanders and Hainault invested a significant portion of their wealth to establish secular coeducational schools (primarily for children) in their realm to teach reading, writing, and simple mathematics. Countess Joan believed that educated adults were a boon to the economy as they could make more money, thus spend more money, and so grow tax revenues. Beguines benefited from this increased literacy, both in their own education and in establishing schools as a chosen ministry.

Recognizing that a better-educated merchant class elsewhere meant growing competition, leading merchants and aristocratic rulers in northern Europe and northern Italy echoed the example of the two countesses. Literacy rose overall, creating a demand for books and venues for the discussion of ideas. This same merchant class was involved in the increased trade with peoples and cultures overseas, particularly Persia and China. Cross-fertilization of ideas and possibilities was proving to be economically profitable—and beguines benefited from the broadening horizon of knowledge.

A major intellectual shift in Europe happened in the 1100s when universities began to separate from the great monastery and cathedral schools; the universities at Bologna, Paris, and Oxford were among the first to be established. While women were not permitted to attend university, beguines invited academic teachers to their homes, and so the latter were exposed to the inquisitive intellect of beguines. Some academics became ardent supporters of the beguines, while others turned into their lifelong enemies.

Many women became beguines as a result of their newfound literacy. Searching for biblical and other spiritual texts in the vernacular, beguines met to study and debate the meaning of these texts. They read theology, homilies, and letters in the vernacular (and sometimes also in Latin). Popular sermons and well-written tracts were copied and disseminated among beguines.

An increasingly educated laity demanded effective preaching from religious leaders. Followers of the vita apostolica had grown intolerant of lax and mediocre preaching, especially from clerics whose private lives were a disaster. These women and men expected intelligent and powerful sermons that challenged them to deeper holiness and called for reform within church and society. Beguines had enormous impact in the church by promoting good preaching, and their approval of specific teachers created opportunities for the Dominicans and Franciscans. One of the most effective writers to use the power of the pen in order to challenge corrupt politicians and church leaders—and he spared no one—was Dante (1265–1321) in *The Divine Comedy*. Many beguines would do the same, in mystical utterances and in their preaching, and one of the most famous of them was Mechthild of Magdeburg.

With the rise of the troubadours in the late eleventh century developed a lifestyle and art form called *fine amour* or *amour courtoise*, courtly love. It spread from southern France across Europe and enjoyed great popularity for two hundred years or more. Troubadours (some of whom were women) wrote, collected, and performed lyrics that glorified love and raised it to spiritual and metaphorical heights of honor, much in the tradition of the biblical Song of Songs. Beguines expanded this notion of "the heart's yearning for the beloved" to express the human search for God, and the beguine Hadewijch is considered the master par excellence in expressing her mystical visions and teachings with the language of courtly love.

While few writings by women mystics from before 1200 have survived, we can assume that earlier women also enjoyed rich mystical experiences of the Divine. After 1200, across Europe, an explosion of recorded mystical experiences of women occurred and was actively shared, and people sought out these women for their spiritual power. Among their followers were educated men who felt no shame in acknowledging these women as their spiritual teachers.

Such spiritual friendships between women and men led to a collaboration in ministry and set an example that encouraged deepening spiritual lives. But these friendships also aroused deep suspicion. Could men and women work side by side without sliding into sexual sin? Could women teach men? And was it safe to teach women theology or Scripture? One famous friendship was that of Francis of Assisi (c. 1181–1226) and Clare of Assisi (c. 1193–1254), who together—despite interference from the papacy—reminded the church of "Lady Poverty," radical love, and profound simplicity. Among other examples of spiritual friendships were those of Angela of Foligno and Brother Arnaldo, Mechthild of Magdeburg and Heinrich of Halle, Catherine of Siena and Raymond of Capua, Lutgard of Aywières and Thomas of Cantimpré; and, perhaps most influentially, there was the deep bond between Marie d'Oignies, often considered the first beguine, and Jacques de Vitry, a future cardinal.

2

BEGUINES
ACROSS EUROPE

MARIE D'OIGNIES (Mary of Oignies) was held in high esteem by beguines and other followers of the vita apostolica, but also by church authorities. So honored was Marie that beguines referred to her as "the first beguine."

The town of Nivelles (south of Brussels) was a spiritual crossroads for the vita apostolica. Born in 1177 to wealthy parents, Marie grew up in the midst of cultural and spiritual vibrancy. She rejected the fine clothing and other adornments offered by her parents, and her simplicity of lifestyle upset them. Despite her familiarity with the Cistercians (the most popular monastic reform movement in the twelfth century), Marie chose not to enter a Cistercian monastery, which would have been an acceptable path for daughters from well-off families. When she was fourteen, her parents arranged a marriage to John, the son of another wealthy Nivelles family. Once married and away from her parents' scrutiny, Marie began a more arduous ascet-ical observance of fasting, prayer, and almsgiving. After a few months of marriage, John experienced a conversion in which he came to desire a deeper relationship with God. Marie and John enjoyed one another's company, and they framed their married life around a daily routine of prayer, fasts, physical labor, and works of charity. Soon the two decided, as was common among followers of the vita apostolica, to live together as brother and sister, eschewing sexual relations. Instead they focused their pas-sion and energies on serving God.

Eventually, Marie and John abandoned their home in Nivelles and moved to nearby Willambroux, where an informal community following the vita apostolica lived alongside lepers. John's brother, Master Guido, served as chaplain of the local church. With other residents of this community, Marie and John fed and bathed lepers, cared for other sick and destitute people, studied, taught children, provided religious instruction, and sat together in prayer. Marie's dedication to serving the poor and to prayer gained renown, and she was becoming known as a "living saint." People flocked from around the region to meet her and speak with her. (We know nothing further about John.)

Marie earned a reputation for the efficacious power of her prayer. She was regarded as having the ability to read souls, which meant that she could gaze upon a person and effectively identify the status of their salvation: was the seeker in a state of sin, or guilty of unconfessed sins? Marie's intent was to heal a person spiritually by calling them to repentance.

Attracting crowds from nearby towns and cities, Marie became increasingly distressed as people constantly sought her out, interrupting her ministry with the lepers. She yearned for a more intense life of prayer and solitude and thus moved in 1207 to a cell near the priory of St. Nicholas in Oignies (a village in southern Belgium). She deepened her life of fasting and prayer while living there as a recluse, but also met with individuals for spiritual counseling and sent words of exhortation to those whose lives needed correction.

Around 1208, the theologian Jacques de Vitry (James of Vitry; c. 1160–1240) arrived from Paris in order to meet Marie, and eventually became her disciple. At Marie's encouragement he briefly returned to Paris to be ordained (in 1210), and then continued his life and ministry at Oignies, serving lepers and the destitute. He referred to Marie as his magistra.

Marie and Jacques became close spiritual friends, exhorting each other toward a deep interior life and in their ministry. Vitry was becoming a popular preacher and Marie urged him to share this gift freely; his fame also grew among church authorities and she encouraged him, despite his resistance, to accept growing responsibilities within the church.

In 1213, when it became evident that Marie was dying (probably due to her long, harsh fasts), she was moved outside her cell into the open air to join in the celebration of mass and the Divine Office. She was no longer able to speak or move on her own. Members of Oignies's spiritual community sat and prayed with her. During vespers one day her friends noticed that Marie's eyes had fixed their gaze toward the sky and that her countenance had begun to brighten with serenity. She smiled and began to sing softly and in a low voice.[1]

Over several days her friends reported that Marie moved between experiencing raptures; praying; sharing her teachings on the Trinity, the Virgin Mary, sections of Scripture; and singing Mary's Magnificat. Her deathbed sermon, which summed up her life's teachings, was recorded by Jacques de Vitry and no doubt shaped by him for the edification of future seekers. This was a common and respected practice in medieval times: a biographer would sum up an important person's life teachings in the form of a deathbed sermon. But it was rare that this was done for a woman.

Marie d'Oignies died in 1213, reportedly on the feast day of John the Baptist. Was this another biographical device by Vitry? John the Baptist, cousin of Jesus of Nazareth, was portrayed by gospel writers as a prophet come to proclaim the arrival of the messiah. John the Baptist was also a favorite saint of followers of the vita apostolica. Was Vitry positioning Marie d'Oignies as a herald of the medieval vita apostolica?

After her death, Marie's many followers—strangers, friends, students, and admirers—spread word of her remarkable life and teachings across Europe. Even Francis of Assisi was said to be one of her admirers, hoping to travel across the Alps to meet her, a dream he was unable to fulfill. Marie's fame and the stories about her life motivated women to imitate her example as beguines.

Jacques de Vitry composed his *Life of Marie d'Oignies* after her death as an argument in support of the beguines whom he had observed in his travels. He regarded beguines as exemplars of the apostolic life and as a bulwark against heresies threatening the church, and encouraged his audience to follow their example. After preaching the Albigensian Crusade (against the heretic Albigensians, or Cathars, in the south of France) as well as the Fifth Crusade, Vitry was chosen as bishop of Acre in the Holy Land. He served there from 1216 onward for a number of years while staying deeply involved in European church and political affairs. In 1229 he became a cardinal and served in Rome. After his death in 1240, he was buried in Oignies, to be near the tomb of Marie.

Marie d'Oignies's devotional life was both typical and extraordinary for a woman of her day. She experienced vivid spiritual images—of Mary, of Jesus, of various saints, and of souls in purgatory—and was skilled in interpreting the meaning behind many of these visions. Sometimes these visions were meant as messages for people she knew; sometimes they were warnings or an indication that she needed to pray for someone "headed for hell" if they did not turn their lives around. And sometimes she was praying for the release of someone from purgatory. With Marie began the belief that beguines held power on behalf of other people over purgatory and hell.

In prayer Marie would so intensely imagine the earthly Jesus as being present that she reported experiencing his presence physically. Vitry shaped these experiences in his *Life of Marie d'Oignies* to coincide with liturgical feasts being celebrated: near the Nativity she embraced the infant Jesus, at the time of the Presentation in the Temple she envisioned Jesus as a young boy, and she saw him as the dying Lord on the cross on Good Friday (but also on Sundays during mass). This biographical device served both to teach Vitry's readers about the power and efficacy of prayer as well as to reinforce gospel stories, making them more vivid.

Marie spent hours in meditation before the consecrated host and experienced Christ's presence in the eucharist as if sitting with an intimate friend. The medieval Catholic Church taught the concept of transubstantiation, meaning that the host made of unleavened wheat bread, when consecrated during mass, would become the Body of Christ. Beginning with Marie, medieval women heavily influenced the developing theology of the eucharist that still impacts today's Catholic Church. Vitry presented Marie's teachings on the power of the eucharist when he wrote her biography. In a statement that was often repeated in medieval Europe, Marie was quoted as saying, "Let the heretic infidels [meaning, false teachers and nonbelievers] be ashamed who receive the delights of this food [the eucharist] neither in the heart nor with faith."[2] She was challenging Christians to understand and believe what happened at the altar during mass, and especially to recognize Christ whom they were receiving in the eucharist.

The Christian Scriptures speak of gifts of the Holy Spirit, the belief that a person can be inspired and endowed by God for particular ministries. Marie most valued that gift of the Holy Spirit called the Spirit of Wisdom, the ability to perceive and understand God's ways or divine intentions. She expressed this gift with the sensuous and very human images of tasting, eating, drinking, mystical inebriation, and insatiable hunger. The beguine mystics Hadewijch and Mechthild of Magdeburg, among others, followed Marie's example of expressing key aspects of the spiritual journey as well as deeply valued spiritual gifts through sensuous images.

Marie embodied the aspirations and values of those who embraced the vita apostolica, and she inspired clerics and theology students toward a more humane and spirit-inspired life. A liturgical commemoration was developed celebrating her life and teachings. The Office for Mary d'Oignies sung at the town of Villers (near Nivelles) in the 1230s and 1240s commemorated her as the initiator of this new beguine way of life.

The growing urban centers of the Low Countries witnessed a proliferation of beguines, many directly inspired by the example of Marie d'Oignies and her early companions (in Oignies itself, a court beguinage existed since 1239). Beguines lived in many towns and cities where they enjoyed ample opportunity to engage in business, thereby supporting themselves and ministering among the poor and vulnerable. Beguines also enjoyed learning from, and debating with, the many talented and gifted preachers passing through these urban areas.

Some beguines in the Low Countries were given direct financial support and political protection by Countess Joan and her sister, Countess Margaret. The countesses also formally established court beguinages in several of the cities of their realm—including Brugge, Douai, Ghent, Kortrijk, and Lille[3]—enabling the local beguines to live and minister with greater freedom. Legal documents provide a record of the many beguinages established in the Low Countries and elsewhere. In 1233, Countess Joan gave official sanction to a group of beguines, formally establishing the court beguinage of St. Elizabeth in Ghent.[4] This beguinage would grow to somewhere between 610 and 730 beguines by 1284. The court beguinage of Cantimpré in Cambrai (northern France) was also established in 1233, while many smaller convents were established in the early to mid-1200s. The city of Aachen had two court beguinages—St. Mathias, established in 1230, and St. Stephen, dating from 1261—along with smaller convents.

Brugge, a major hub of the textile industry, had a number of communities of beguines. As mentioned, the court beguinage Wijngaard (also known as St. Elizabeth) was established around 1242; a smaller court beguinage called Ter Hooie (and dedicated to the Blessed Virgin Mary) was established before 1262. In Brussels, the court beguinage Wijngaard was established around 1247, and the smaller convents of Ter Arken and Meerbeek began there in 1263 and 1272, respectively. The court beguinage of St. Catherine in Diest (near Leuven) was founded in 1245, and a smaller convent in the same town was established in 1251.

In the year 1240, the court beguinage of St. Christine took root in Ieper (Ypres; near Lille), with several smaller convents established there between 1271 and 1323. The court beguinage of St. Elizabeth in Valenciennes (not far from Cambrai) began in 1239. In Tournai (near Lille), the court beguinage of St.

Elizabeth (also known as Des Prés) was started in 1241, and the court beguinage of St. Catherine in Tongeren (near Maastricht) two years later. Namur had a court beguinage as of 1235 and the smaller convent of St. Symphorien as of 1248. The large court beguinage dedicated to the Virgin Mary and St. Catherine was established in Mechelen (north of Brussels) in 1245—eventually it would house between 1,500 and 1,900 beguines—and the smaller court beguinage of St. Mary Magdalen in 1259. The court beguinage of Ten Hove in Leuven was established around 1232, and about 1,270 women lived there at one point. Maastricht's court beguinage of St. Catherine began in 1251 and the smaller convent of St. Andrew in 1264.

Among the earliest and most prolific centers for beguines was the city of Liège, where they lived and served until the mid-1800s. The biography of the widow Odilia, written after her death in 1220, preserves the record of the early beguine development there. Odilia lived a life of service to others and of intense prayer. Around 1203 she began experiencing ecstatic visions, like Marie d'Oignies, while gazing upon the elevated host during mass. Her biographer reported that Odilia saw Jesus as an infant and images of his suffering and Crucifixion while the priest raised the host.

Between 1207 and 1219, women in Liège began to gather in homes near the church of St. Christophe; by 1241 a beguinage had formed that would number around a thousand beguines in the mid-1300s.[5] Odilia's son, John, who served as chaplain at the Cathedral of St. Lambert in Liège, donated a house for twenty-four local beguines shortly before his death in 1241.

In Marie d'Oignies's hometown of Nivelles, two thousand beguines were reportedly living between 1256 and 1263. St. Syr, the most famous beguinage in Nivelles, had fifty-one women by

1284. A group of beguines near the church of St. Sépulchre in Nivelles operated a hospital and a school for local children.

Ida of Nivelles (1199–1231), who would one day become a famous Cistercian nun, ran away from home when she was nine years old, taking with her only her Psalter, which she had begun to memorize. She joined a group of beguines and continued her education with them. Six years later, she joined the Cistercian monastery at Kerkom, soon moving to the Cistercian monastery at La Ramée, but remained in contact with her beguine friends.

Ida was remembered as a friend of beguines as well as their defender against critics; and beguines upheld Ida as one of their own because of her life example and teachings. Ida felt deep compassion for the struggles of others. Like Marie d'Oignies, she spent hours in contemplative prayer in front of the consecrated eucharist and emotionally entered into the experiences of Jesus's suffering and death (this was a revered path of prayer). Ida was renowned for her ability to discern the state of another person's soul and served as confessor to many. Perceived to be a powerful intercessor, she became known as "the Compassionate" because of her deep care for souls suffering the torments of purgatory.

The town of Huy (between Namur and Liège) had upwards of nineteen beguine communities (the first of them was started around 1251), and they each had from three to seventeen members. One beguinage there lasted until the French Revolution. Among the many beguines of Huy was a widow named Juetta. Born in 1158, Juetta was only eighteen when her husband died and she was left to raise two children on her own. Five years later, she left her home and children (a common and accepted practice in the Middle Ages) in order to serve lepers at an old chapel across the river Meuse from the town gates of Huy. Gradually, Juetta expanded the humble facilities into a well-equipped hospital with a lovely chapel and additional living space for beguines. This complex would eventually be called the hospital of Grands Malades.

After ten years of ministry, Juetta sought greater solitude for her prayer. She had herself walled in as an anchoress in a cell connected to the lepers' chapel, and she lived there until her death in 1228. (Seeking such solitude was not unusual among beguines. They saw no contradiction between times of intense prayer and times of active ministry.) Juetta was a mystic who reported receiving visions of Mary and Jesus, and she offered spiritual direction and counseling to many. At times she ordered powerful men to the window of her cell—and these men so respected and revered Juetta that they appeared as she demanded—in order to challenge their behavior. Juetta was remembered for her spiritual authority, an authority she was not reluctant to exercise.

In 1255, King Louis IX of France (Saint Louis) visited the court beguinage St. Elizabeth in Ghent. Impressed with what he witnessed, the king established the court beguinage St. Catherine in Paris around 1260. Its first grand mistress was Agnès d'Orchies from Flanders, and the community flourished for several centuries. Despite this safe and comfortable option, some of the beguines of Paris continued to live in their own homes or in family homes. The Paris beguinages operated schools for children, cared for the sick, and engaged in commercial business. Beguines both inside and outside St. Catherine had diverse occupations and businesses, and they enjoyed ties to wealthy Parisian merchants and even to the royal family.

Between 1245 and 1355, fifteen beguinages were established in Douai. One of them was the court beguinage of Champfleury (also called St. Elizabeth) that grew to include at least one hundred beguines. Its hospital flourished, and from 1300 onward Champfleury's chapel also functioned as a parish church.

Other towns and cities in northern France where beguines lived included Arras, St. Omer, and Lille. Arras at one time had nine beguinages, and in one of them lived seventy-two beguines. St. Omer had up to twenty-one beguine convents, with 395 women living there by 1322. Lille was home to only one known community of beguines, St. Elizabeth, which was located outside the gates of St. Peter. St. Elizabeth was established around 1244, growing into one of the largest beguinages in Europe. In 1413 the beguines there began a major renovation of their chapel that continued until at least 1450.

Colette of Corbie (1381–1447) was born to elderly parents in Corbie (near Amiens) who died when she was an adolescent. She joined the beguines of her hometown but eventually yearned for a stricter observance of ascetic practices. She chose the Poor Clares and then became a recluse. Visions, however, kept pressing her to take on the reform of the Franciscans. In one vision, she saw a tree growing into her anchorhold; in another vision, Francis of Assisi visited her. After resisting this call at first, she finally relented and began a politically astute movement. By the time of her death, Colette had reformed seven communities of Franciscan men and established (or reformed) seventeen women's communities, which were mostly in the Poor Clare tradition.

Colette lived a quietly austere life even in the midst of her extensive reform work and allegedly continued to have many visions, experienced levitation in prayer, prophesied, and had the ability to read others' conscience. Much of the fruit of her prayers and visions were recorded and put to the service of her reformist mission.

Beguines in southern France lived and worked both in cities and in small towns. Like beguines in the Low Countries, they wove cloth, a few of them were involved in banking and trade, and they were great preachers, too, deeply concerned with the call to reform a corrupt church. Some of them lived among lepers. One exemplar beguine was Douceline of Digne (c. 1215–1274). She was born into a devout merchant family in the town of Digne in Provence. When her mother died, the family moved to Hyères (near the Mediterranean) to be near Douceline's brother, Hugues (Hugh) of Digne, a well-known Franciscan.

After some years of caring for the poor and sick from her family's home, Douceline made a commitment as a beguine around 1238. As an increasing number of women associated themselves with her, she established a beguine community outside Hyères in about 1241. Later she established a second house within Hyères, thus closer to the Franciscan church the beguines attended. Around 1250 she also started a beguine community in Marseille, leading the communities in both places until her death.

Like many beguine mystics, Douceline experienced repeated ecstatic moments in prayer; she also fell into ecstasy when receiving the eucharist. Those around her reported that at times Douceline wept copiously, either in sorrow for those whose lives were headed for destruction or in joy for the love of God. Witnesses claimed to have seen her levitate—the phenomenon of rising off the ground or floating in the air—during prayer.

In contrast to the struggle for power and approval that marked her social class, Douceline prized the lowly, humble place in society. When her followers expressed concern that Douceline was treated with contempt by her detractors, she responded: "Truly, it is my honor and my glory, my joy and my crown that the world holds us in great scorn, and that everyone disdains us."[6] Challenging a church and society burdened with a rigid social system, Douceline encouraged her fellow beguines to ignore the worry about one's place and reputation in society in favor of serving the gospel; they would find freedom by not caring about what others thought of them.

Douceline and her group endured suspicion and contempt because they lived without male supervision and, worse, dared to be their own spiritual authority. By letting go of any concern for status and reputation, they could live with greater inner freedom and pursue ministries as they chose. Douceline and her fellow beguines lived at a time when followers of the vita apostolica in Provence exercised a particularly ardent devotion to the Holy Spirit. Mystical phenomena associated with the influence of the Holy Spirit were reported throughout the region.

Some beguines and Franciscans in the south of France were suspect because, in their ministry to marginalized people, they may have associated with the heretical Cathars. But Douceline spoke out in defense of such beguines and Franciscans who, in her understanding, were faithful to their call to serve the very poorest and to preach reform in the church.

Douceline was loved for being a steady source of strength in the midst of the social, political, and religious upheaval of her day. With her genuine spiritual power, her popularity as an efficacious preacher, her connections within the church and also with Charles of Anjou, brother of King Louis IX, Douceline provided stability. It is believed that Philippine Porcellet, Lady of Artignols, a beguine from a powerful aristocratic family of Provence, wrote down Douceline's *Life*.

Lay religious women in Italy led independent lives committed to serving God and the poor much like the beguines in northern Europe. Known by such names as penitentia, bizzocha, or pinzochera, they lived alone or in small groups, gathered for prayer in a local chapel or church, may have followed an informal rule, were self-supporting, and served the sick and destitute.

As in other parts of Europe, these Italian women at times sought out Dominican or Franciscan friars as spiritual guides, or associated themselves with other laypeople in the so-called Third Orders (or tertiaries) of the Franciscans and Dominicans.

Francesca Bussa dei Ponziani (1384–1440), later known as Francesca Romana (Frances of Rome), was remembered with love and admiration by her contemporaries, and testimony gathered in the years after her death revealed a quiet mystic with healing powers. She and her husband, Lorenzo dei Ponziani, were members of the Roman nobility. Her mother frequented a Roman church served by the Benedictine monks of Monte Oliveto (Tuscany). Francesca and her sister-in-law, Vannozza, were active followers of the vita apostolica. Besides running their household and caring for family, Francesca and Vannozza attended mass, begged alms for the sick and poor, and worked at the hospital of Santo Spirito. Begging for them was a penance, since it was considered shameful for members of the nobility to beg.

Francesca, Lorenzo, and Vannozza lived through famines and pestilence that heavily afflicted the people of Rome. They opened their home to the sick and destitute after the hospitals had filled up. During the decades referred to as the Great Schism of the West (1378–1417), when several powerful men claimed the papacy as their own, battles raged on the streets of Rome among the warring papal supporters and the city was occupied by opposing factions. As a result, Francesca and Lorenzo lost all their wealth.

Her contemporaries believed Francesca had the divine gift of healing. (During the papal hearings that considered her case for canonization, over sixty cases of healing were reported and attributed to her.) She herself fell sick with the plague in 1414 and began experiencing profound visions. After she had recovered, she continued nursing sick people in her home as well as in their own dwellings.

Women, mostly of the nobility, gathered around Francesca, continuing to live in their own homes, meeting for prayer, and serving the sick and destitute. Eventually, some of her followers bought a large house and began living as a community. In 1436, after the death of her husband, Francesca was asked by her friends and followers to serve as magistra. These Roman lay religious women never became nuns, wore lay garments, and moved freely in society to pursue their ministry. They were very popular, even accepted by church authorities. Many women and men joined Francesca's quiet and unassuming way of life and shared in her work among the poor.

Francesca influenced a lay movement in Rome that exists to this day, a community of oblates connected to the Benedictines of Monte Oliveto. Canonized in 1608, Francesca Romana is considered the patron saint of Benedictine oblates, and Santa Francesca Romana, an old church near the Roman Forum, is dedicated to her.

In the early thirteenth century, Clare of Assisi had likewise decided to dedicate her life to a radical and uncompromising following of the gospel. Francis and his companions received her promise of dedication in the little chapel of St. Maria degli Angeli (the Porziuncula) outside Assisi. Francis cut off her hair and welcomed her as one of their own.

Clare sought a radical gospel way of simplicity, wishing to live with the poor and rejected of society. As an act of personal asceticism, she became a penitentia servant to the nearby monastery of women at San Paolo in Bastia. She soon left this monastery, feeling the call to a more radical poverty. She moved to Sant' Angelo, a house of fellow penitentiae women in Panzo. But Clare's powerful family in Assisi diligently sought to disturb her new way of life. The renown of the spiritual power of Clare and Francis also caught the attention of Pope Innocent III. The double pressure of family and pope meant Clare was eventually forced to live in an enclosed community at San Damiano outside Assisi—much to her personal sadness. Clare of Assisi's followers were later given the name Poor Clares.

Clare and Francesca were not unique in medieval Italy. Women formed loose alliances in many cities, including Milan and Pisa, Perugia and Rome. They strove to follow "the poor and humble Christ," sharing the life of the poor through manual labor and attending to the suffering around them. Medieval Italian chronicles give witness to an abundance of penitentiae, many of whom were identified by their contemporaries as mystics, including Chiara of Montefalco (1268–1308) and Catherine of Siena (1347–1380). Umiltà of Faenza (1226–1310), Margaret of Cortona (1247–1297), and Angela of Foligno (1248–1309) were some of the famous Italian spiritual women who preached and called on their audiences to reform their lives. Some of their writings have survived over the centuries.

The bizzoche and pinzochere favored quiet, informal living arrangements. They frequently remained in their own homes or those of their families, sometimes living in twos and threes. These women gathered in local churches for mass and prayer, but they also often established independent oratories or chapels—to gain the freedom to pray in a manner of their own choosing. Their own chapel provided some level of autonomy from well-meaning but interfering family and also from church leadership.

The bizzoche and pinzochere were fiercely independent. While they might serve in institutions such as hospitals and leprosariums, they rarely, unlike beguines in northern Europe, established or administered these institutions. They preferred not to be tied down to one ministry, but rather to move freely about and to do differing works of charity as needed.

These women were not always successful in preserving their independence, but they did not want to be subsumed into monastic orders or the emerging mendicants.[7] However, a number of Italian penitentiae were attracted to the charism of the Dominicans and Franciscans. While the Dominican Order formally welcomed only men, many penitentiae—including Catherine of Siena—chose to follow the Dominican spirit with its commitment to study, teaching, and preaching. But when chroniclers claimed bizzoche in one region of Italy as Franciscan tertiaries, many of these very women denied this claim and went about their lives and ministries as before.

In 1213, three women of Padua lived as a small group of penitentiae, dedicating their lives to prayer, fasting, and serving the poor. More women came to gather around them. Those members of the group who could read recited the seven canonical hours, while the illiterate prayed the Pater Noster (Our Father) and Ave Maria (Hail Mary). By 1225 they embraced St. Cecilia, the patron saint of music, as their patron.

The colorful pinzochera Guglielma of Milan was allegedly a Bohemian princess. Guglielma appeared in Milan sometime in the 1260s, dressed in a plain brown robe, and she associated herself with the Cistercian monks at Chiaravalle. She lived a simple, independent life as a self-proclaimed "widow" in her own home, teaching publicly on the Holy Spirit and acting as a peacemaker among fractious Milanese families. She had many followers but she also became associated with heresy. A posthumous inquisitorial trial was held in Milan in 1300. Found guilty, her bones were exhumed and burned. But not much was resolved, and devotion to Guglielma did not cease.

Umiliana dei Cerchi (1219–1246) was a noble Florentine who had been married off to enhance her family's fortunes. Once widowed, she gave her children to her husband's family, joined a group of local pinzochere, and served the poor. Seeking ever greater solitude, Umiliana moved into a tower owned by her family to live as a recluse, and became a spiritual beacon.

Umiltà of Faenza, a few years younger than Umiliana, came from a noble family in Faenza (near Ravenna). She, too, was forced to marry, but when her children died, Umiltà convinced her husband to part in order for her to live a more dedicated religious life. After several attempts of joining different religious communities, Umiltà lived as a recluse, and fame of her spiritual power grew. Umiltà dictated a series of homilies and spiritual treatises to her disciple, Margaret of Faenza, that were shared among monastic communities, and she eventually also founded a monastery in Florence.

The life of Angelina of Montegiove (c. 1357–1435) serves as an important transition point in the convoluted relationship between Italian lay religious women and Franciscan men who were seeking to control women associated with the Franciscan ideal. Born into a noble family in Umbria, Angelina at one point became attracted to the spiritual life and, in about 1394, joined a very active lay religious community called Sant'Anna in Foligno (near Assisi). These women gathered for mass and prayer in their chapel and served the local poor and sick. With Angelina's creative and charismatic leadership, the number of women grew to the point that several other communities were established.

Seeking to care for her followers and to defend their individual charism, Angelina obtained the right to conduct the visitations of each of her communities and was named their "minister general" in 1428 by Pope Martin V. The leadership of the Franciscans sought to place all Third Order women and men under their own authority. Angelina again prevailed with an affirmation from the pope for her community's lifestyle. But the issue of authority of her federated communities (and other tertiaries) and, specifically for the women, the issue of enclosure would cause turmoil for many years.

Agnes Blannbekin (c. 1244–1315) was the daughter of farmers, probably from the village of Plambach (near Vienna). She could read but not write, which was quite common for her day. She went to live in Vienna, a city with many beguines. Like other free-spirited beguines of her day, Agnes moved freely about Vienna, pausing several times a day to pray in shrines and attend mass at different churches. One of her devotional practices was to approach an altar after she had attended mass (and after, she assumed, the priest and fellow worshipers had departed) and kiss the altar with a great display of emotion, sometimes even dancing around it with joy. She thus treated the eucharist as a close friend and revered king, and she also made a conscious statement of disobedience: she was approaching the space around the altar, an act forbidden to women in medieval times.

Agnes reported that in one of her visions Jesus had told her that "a person can neither work for nor grow toward grace through continuous physical efforts. Therefore the seeker should always remain in a mental state of desire for an increase in grace, and in this, the seeker makes progress. And whenever desire quiets down, then progress in grace quiets down, and when desire decreases, so goes grace."[8]

Agnes was ridiculed for her apparently odd behavior, much like Douceline of Digne or Francis of Assisi. For example, one day witnesses saw her bowing to a basement window as she passed by. Her detractors later discovered that a stolen consecrated host had

41

been kept in that basement room. Her biographer attributed her behavior to divine knowledge: Agnes had sensed that Christ was present in that consecrated host.

Agnes's *Life and Revelations*, written by her confessor, provides a panorama of Viennese religious life at the time. She was ardent in chastising fellow beguines whose religious observance she deemed lax, as well as nuns and priests she found wanting. Her confessor acknowledged her as one of his own teachers, both for her spiritual insights and for her theological sophistication.

In the German-speaking part of Europe, beguines tended to live in smaller groups. Urban areas in these German regions also tended to have more beguine convents than in the Low Countries. In Strasbourg, for example, beguine convents housed an average of ten women, while the average number was seven women in Cologne, and three to four in Mainz. Parishes in northwest Germany (close to the Low Countries) commonly included two or more beguine communities.

Documents show that by 1223, beguines existed in Cologne. Two sisters, named Elizabeth and Sophie, sold properties, and this sale was legally recorded, identifying the sisters as beguines. The English Benedictine monk and chronicler Matthew Paris initially held beguines in contempt, seriously doubting their ability to follow the vita apostolica. But his opinion changed and he came to respect their frugal lifestyle, their commitment to manual labor and to simplicity of life. In 1243 Matthew wrote in his chronicle that two thousand beguines lived in and around Cologne, which was a major medieval city. By the end of the fourteenth century, Cologne hosted 160 beguine convents. Around Münster (in Westphalia), large growth in beguine foundations occurred between 1250 and 1350, with new foundations recorded through the 1400s.

Like their Italian counterparts, a significant number of

beguines in the German realm were attracted to the teaching and preaching charism of the Dominicans. While Italian women who followed the Dominican spirit remained penitentiae, German beguines began to call themselves Dominican. Frequently, these German beguines had been chastised by the male Dominican leadership for calling themselves Dominican—the men did not want these women in their order—but the women remained resolute. By the 1300s, Dominican women in Germany were reluctantly acknowledged, having formerly been beguine communities. (Many present-day Dominican sisters in the United States and Germany recognize their beguine roots in medieval Germany.)

The religious laywomen of the Iberian peninsula—the beatas—emerged around 1200,[9] like the beguines elsewhere in Europe. The sixteenth-century historian Alonso Morgado claimed that beatas had been an established tradition in Seville "since time immemorial."[10] Beatas lived independent lives, often in their own homes. When beatas lived in small groups, their home was called a *beaterio*. Those beatas recognized for their spiritual leadership were called *madre*. Much of our information regarding beatas comes from the detailed records of the Spanish Inquisition, which unfortunately confiscated most of the writings of beatas. (Scholars are still searching for these writings.) A book called *Aviso*, written for beatas by their contemporary Diego Pérez de Valdivia (1525–1589), also provides some information. Beatas were fiercely independent, resisting attempts to force them into traditional religious houses. Their informal connection to the church was usually through their confessor.[11] While their attire was similar to beguines in its practicality and simplicity, beatas, like most Spanish women at the time, wore a veil in public.

Like the beguines in northern Europe, Spanish beatas came from every social group: some began this religious lifestyle as adolescents and others as widows, some chose it because they could not afford the required dowry for marriage or for a more traditional monastery, and nearly all worked for their own support and to support their hospitals and other ministries. For example, records indicate that by the later fifteenth century, beatas offered a significant ministry to women in prison: preaching to them, teaching them skills so that they could support themselves after their release, and providing places to stay for women newly released from prison.

María García (1340–1426) was born in Toledo to noble parents. As a precocious child she would go to a secret place to pray and would gather the leftovers from the family table to give to the poor. In her adolescence, she and her companion, the widow Mayor Gomez, would beg alms (against their families' wishes) in the streets of Toledo—even in the cathedral—on behalf of the poor. Desiring to escape their lascivious king, Pedro I, María and Mayor fled to Talavera (southwest of Madrid). Their new home would become known as Santa María de la Sisla. In 1369, after King Pedro had been murdered, María and Mayor returned to Toledo and joined other beatas in their ministry to the poor and in prayer. With her inheritance, María was able to purchase a home for the beatas and named it San Pablo. She spent her later years exhorting the women of Toledo to a more simple and prayerful life, and also helped to establish religious houses and supported the poor.

Catalina Guiera,[12] a wealthy widow in Ávila who had lived as a beata since her husband's death, dictated her will in 1463 and made detailed arrangements endowing several of her homes for the ongoing support of fellow beatas. In 1478 this group of beatas chose to become Dominican.

María de Ajofrín, who also lived in the 1400s, was from the town of Ajofrín near Toledo. She had a vision at the age of fifteen that inspired her to join the beatas at San Pablo. It was said that she continued to receive visions and prophecies, most of them centered on the need for church reform. The most significant vision that she reported happened in 1484, when Christ ordered María to instruct the archbishop of Toledo to eradicate the five sins of immoral clerics that were "daily crucifying Christ": lack of faith, greed, lust, ignorance, and insufficient reverence for sacred things. The "evidence" that gave authority to her vision were the stigmata that María was alleged to have received—in her case, a lance mark on her breast. Stigmata served as a sign of direct authority from God, and in María's case, Archbishop Mendoza listened and a reform movement began.

María de Toledo (1437–after 1484) was born to noble parents and was married against her will. Widowed without children, she associated herself with some local Franciscans and began to live the life of a beata. With her companion, Juana Rodriguez, she visited the sick, provided dowries for orphans, fed and clothed the poor, and paid the debts of those in prison. She also culti-vated a deeply contemplative life, including living as a recluse for a year. Apparently she received many visions and revelations. With her family's wealth, María eventually established a hospital where she, along with her companions, helped to care for the sick. She nearly died from illness, too, probably something she had contracted while caring for patients. Some years after recov-ering, María used her fortune to establish a convent for Francis-can tertiaries, and in 1484 she herself became a Poor Clare.

María Dávila, who came from Ávila and had been twice wid-owed without children, joined twelve other beatas in Calaba-zanos (north of Madrid) in 1494. She used her wealth to help establish several religious houses and rebuilt several shrines. In her will, written in 1502, she directed that any of her possessions left at the time of her death be given to establish a new Poor Clares foundation nearby. She died in 1511.

Mari Díaz (c. 1490–1572) of Vita (northwest of Madrid) was as popular in her lifetime as her contemporary Teresa de Jesús, better known today as Teresa of Ávila. Mari lived as a beata against her parents' wishes, serving the poor when not working on the family's prosperous farm. She moved to Ávila in the 1530s, after her parents had died, in search of better sermons. She intentionally lived in one of the poor neighborhoods and quickly developed a reputation for her many hours spent in prayer, the extreme simplicity of her lifestyle, and her generosity toward her neighbors. With some reluctance she accepted a request that she move into the palace of a devout widow. While she missed her free lifestyle and endured taunts from the palace staff, her reputation for common sense, wisdom, and spiritual power grew in Ávila. Soon she was given the honorific title of madre. She was asked to resolve family disputes, and she was particularly loved by children whom she taught and with whom she spent much of her free time. Mari met Teresa of Ávila at the widow's palace in the 1550s. After Mari moved into a hermitage around 1565, Teresa visited Mari and enjoyed conversations with her. Many people around Ávila came to seek intercessory prayer from Madre Mari, as well as spiritual counsel. Testimony after her death recorded many who claimed that the prayers of Mari had healed illnesses and cured infertility.

By the sixteenth and seventeenth centuries, thousands of women lived as beatas, attracted to a life of independent prayer and ministry. Despite their generous outreach to the poor, beatas came under increasing scrutiny for their independence, which was perceived as a lack of allegiance to the institutional church. They found themselves under investigation by the Inquisition, which sought to destroy their credibility. A major concern of the church hierarchy was to curb beatas who had developed so much influence among the laity, independent of ecclesiastical oversight.

Beguines in Scandinavia followed a somewhat independent path from beguines in other parts of Europe. Scandinavian beguines lived outside towns and cities and near men's monasteries. They, like beguines elsewhere, established and maintained infirmaries for the poor. We have records of Danish beguines being present in Roskilde from the 1260s onward, in Copenhagen since the 1270s, and in Ribe (on the North Sea) since the 1290s.

The Swedish widow Ingrid of Skänninge (1220–1282), who came from a prominent family, belonged to a group of beguines who dedicated their lives to prayer and serving the poor. In Ingrid's canonization process, her chaplain, the Dominican Peter of Dacia, reported that Ingrid had given up eating meat, rarely drank beer (in general, water was unsafe to drink in medieval times), and seldom consumed dairy products. Peter of Dacia also described some of her powerful mystical experiences. Like other medieval mystics, Ingrid would "allow" herself to experience the Passion of Christ, essentially reliving it on Fridays. This was a form of devotion (wanting to "join a friend" during a horrific time) and a form of preaching. Witnesses reported that Ingrid, when she relived Christ's Passion, would fall into ecstasy, at times even bearing the stigmata and other signs of Christ's suffering on her body.

For the last two years of her life, Ingrid was part of a group of beguines embracing the Dominican charism. By the later 1200s, many Scandinavian beguines had begun to embrace the spirituality of the Dominicans, like their fellow beguines in the German realm. Some Dominican houses of men in Scandinavia extended protection to beguines against a hostile church leadership. At a later time, beguines also found protection living near communities of Birgittine nuns, followers of Birgitta of Sweden (c. 1303–1373).

We have records that Bishop Nicolaus Hermansson of Linköping in 1388 gave permission for the beguines around Vadstena (on Lake Vättern) to continue their lifestyle. Then, in a change of policy, Archbishop Johan in Uppsala in 1412 condemned the presence of beguines at Vadstena, apparently having accepted the rumors that beguines, without men as their superiors, were lazy, drunk, and sexually promiscuous. Yet, as so frequently happened, the archbishop concluded his letter of condemnation by acknowledging that any exemplary beguines—devout, chaste, and living an approved life—were quite acceptable. In this letter the archbishop also ordered the Birgittine nuns at Vadstena to cease aiding or protecting the local beguines. But the Birgittines continued to do so. (Correspondence from Vadstena in 1429 mentions beguines also in Gdańsk, Poland.)

In Scandinavia, as in the Low Countries, persecution of beguines often centered on valuable land. In 1506, the Birgittine monks at Vadstena demanded, under the guise of alleged heresy and questionable morality, the departure of the neighboring beguines. In reality, the monks wanted the land the beguines were living on in order to expand their own gardens.

While laywomen seeking to follow the vita apostolica were a phenomenon that emerged around the same time across medieval Europe, the personal stories of only a small number of these women have been preserved. But we can be certain that thousands of beguines, penitentiae, beatas—and however else these women were called in their hometown or region—walked with passion the path that they felt called to: quietly but forcefully improving the lives of those around them while cultivating an intense spiritual life.

3

THE
BEGUINAGE

IMAGINE YOURSELF VISITING a small city in Flanders around the year 1300. It's an early spring day, and you are strolling along a busy canal with boats carrying goods to and from market. Bustling crowds of people are calling to one another, hawking their wares and services. Animals tended by children jostle for space; carts pulled by oxen pass by. The air is moist and pungent: the sweat of human labor, rotting garbage, and manure mix with the strong odor of fish and seafood. The large canal, hemmed in by hard-packed earth or stone, winds its way through the city. Baskets of herbs and pots of flowers placed alongside pathways and beside doorways give you an occasional breath of decent air. Now you follow a smaller waterway that takes you toward the edge of the city, and you arrive at your destination. Crossing over a stone bridge, you see the sign above the gated entrance that proclaims to all that this beguinage is dedicated to the Virgin Mary. An elderly woman, with thinning white hair peeking out from underneath her gray homespun cap, is sitting inside the gatehouse. She greets you with a nearly toothless smile. After you state your business—visiting a beguine who illuminates books—the gate is opened and you are invited into the *begijnhof*.

Before you lies an expanse of land, graced with trees and walking paths. There are women with hooded capes accompanying frail women, and some are bustling about with baskets of food. Children are chasing a ball. A steep-roofed stone church stands proudly toward your left. Curious, you follow the groomed path to the church, open the heavy wooden double doors, and enter the cool darkness of the sanctuary. Your eyes adjust, and you see many individual chairs, each paired with a wooden desk. Halfway down the nave is an elegant pulpit displaying beautiful carvings. You are surprised. In most churches the pulpit displays the symbols of the four gospel writers—an angel for Matthew, a winged lion for Mark, a winged ox for Luke, and an eagle for John—but here you are greeted by the carved effigies of four women. The beguines chose four women who they felt had proclaimed the gospel for their lives: the apostle Mary Magdalene, the martyrs Saint Catherine of Alexandria and Saint Agnes, and the abbess of Andenne, Begga. You smile with delight.

After you have bowed to the high altar in honor of God and Christ, you leave the church. Your host, who has lived in this community as a beguine for fifteen years, greets you outside, and together you walk to her home. Each house around the perimeter of the beguinage is constructed of brick or stone and has a small private garden in front. There is also a long building, two stories high with a steeply pitched roof, which is finely constructed of wood with a generous placement of windows. This building is a dormitory where beguines of little financial means, or those who choose a simpler lifestyle, dwell. You pass by the path that leads down to the storage barns of the beguinage and a small wharf at the canal. The women ship their completed goods and receive their purchases there. You learn that in cities with a canal system, court beguinages are usually connected to the water so that goods can be delivered and finished products sent out.

You turn a corner and go down a path with newly built homes, wider and taller than the others. Here your host lives and works. You step inside her home and find a room warmed by a stone fireplace—the receiving room. A long wooden table is there, a cupboard filled with pewter plates and drinking cups, and several chairs. Then your host escorts you up steep stairs to the second landing, which has several sleeping spaces. In a corner is a pile of wool. You also notice several spinning wheels. On the third landing is your host's workspace—a room with a large window that invites the sunlight in. A table with jars and brushes and palettes sits on one side of this workroom, and along the window is your host's scripting table, which she can easily move to maximize the sun's rays: she illuminates prayer books and specially ordered Psalters. She receives commissions from local artisans who send her the vellum sheets filled with text awaiting illumination before binding. Some vellum sheets come from monasteries that cannot keep up with demand. She explains to you how she grinds her own colors and mixes powdered gold with raw egg to make her own shell gold; she works with silver, too, but the gold and turquoise are her favorites.

You return to the receiving room on the ground floor. Your host shares her new home with five boarders, all of them fellow beguines. They had wanted a home big enough for all of them to live in, with ample space for their work: spinning, weaving, and other tasks. To make this arrangement happen, your host had to purchase a piece of land adjacent to the beguinage, open a new pathway, and construct her home. She sold the unneeded land to other beguines, who built their own homes. Thus she essentially enlarged the beguinage. You sit down at the wooden table, and both of you enjoy some of the beguines' fine brewed ale and freshly baked biscuits.

The impressive walled beguine complexes we can visit in the Low Countries to this day are called court beguinages (*curtis begijnhoven*). They accounted for about a fourth of medieval beguine communities in that part of Europe. Court beguinages were often built outside the city walls, usually in a field, meadow, marsh, or other land with little economic value (and, whenever possible, with access to a waterway). Wealthy beguines built individual homes of brick or stone, arranged around the outer edge of the beguinage property and facing inward; high walls connecting these homes completed the enclosure. And there was an official entrance gate. Wealthy beguines might live alone or with a few select companions in their homes. They were free to make this choice. Frequently, larger dormitory-style buildings were built to provide housing for beguines of humbler means. Newly arrived beguines usually rented a room in the dormitory or in one of the private homes.

A beguine who owned a private home within the court beguinage agreed that her home would never be turned over to an "outsider." She could leave her home to a fellow beguine, such as a granddaughter or niece, in her will, or could sell her home to another beguine. If a beguine departed the community or was forcibly removed, her home became the property of the court beguinage or of the infirmary.[1] Beguines could purchase a vacated private home if one became available. Funds from the sale or lease of these homes financed their infirmaries (also called hospitals or hospices) and other common buildings.

Court beguinages typically included vegetable gardens and spacious meadows, to keep milk cows, sheep, and goats; henhouses and beehives; a brewery and bakery; and workspace for preparing fleece, spinning, and weaving. One would commonly find a chapel or church there and an infirmary for the sick and the dying. The infirmary, which served poor women (especially poor widows) and children, was considered a beguinage's central and most important institution.

Most court beguinages eventually gained parochial status, meaning they were declared independent parishes by both the local church and secular authorities and assigned their own parish priest. This meant increased independence for the beguinage, and more freedom regarding their choice of artwork, church services, and priests. Sometimes beguines hired their own chaplain (usually a Franciscan or Dominican), even without having parish status—they did so without official permission.

The court beguinage, while not a monastic enclosure, provided a safe area for beguines to live in, earn an income, and minister without interference from unwanted intrusion. Court beguinages functioned as fairly independent villages within (or adjacent to) a town or city, with the women in control—and safe from thieves and marauding gangs. The women were also, for the most part, safe from rape there. Medieval women (including beguines) from prominent families, or who were themselves wealthy, were in danger of rape with the intent of forcing them into a marriage. As appalling as it is to our modern sensibilities, the assailant could go to court and demand the "right" to marry the woman he had raped in order to "clear her reputation."

Enforced marriage, a common problem of the day, was motivated by greed and the hope for improved political connections.

Court beguinages in the Low Countries often grew to be
quite large and essentially self-sufficient, thus becoming known
as a *civitas beghinarum* (city of beguines).[2] One hundred to four
hundred inhabitants was common, but there could be many
more. As mentioned, the court beguinage of St. Elizabeth in
Ghent had been established with the support of Countess Joan
of Flanders and Hainault and built on marshy land outside the
city walls in 1234. By the end of the 1200s, St. Elizabeth had
between 610 and 730 women living there. At the beginning of
the fourteenth century, this beguinage enjoyed two churches,
eighteen dormitories, over one hundred individual houses, a
brewery, an infirmary, a cemetery, and a public square.

One of the oldest court beguinages, St. Christophe in Liège,
numbered around one thousand members by 1253. And St.
Catherine at Mechelen, established in 1245, grew to between
1,500 and 1,900 beguines in the late fifteenth and early sixteenth
centuries.[3] In 1271 the court beguinage at Tongeren included
only a few houses. By 1322 the community had grown to fifty
houses, and each house was named either for the beguine who
built it or for the saint to whom she chose to dedicate her home.

These magnificent court beguinages resulted from several
factors. In addition to the safety and independence beguines
found there, they wanted physical and mental space to support
themselves and the poor, and to earn their livelihood without
disruption or interruption from the broader community. Daily
life within the court beguinage could be arranged according
to their own preferences and priorities. Many early beguines
were quite wealthy and were used to having a "realm" of their
own liking. Court beguinages allowed beguines to shape their
ministry as they saw fit. Beguines enjoyed the active support of

secular authorities because of their payment of taxes and their generous ministry. These women brought a level of stability to a town or city because of their care for the poor, lepers, and the sick, and their education of children. Countesses Joan and Margaret, for example, supported beguines in their realm in different ways. The countesses extended legal protection, provided land for court beguinages, and gave funds for the construction of buildings and the education of children. In 1242, Countess Joan issued a general order to bailiffs and aldermen of Flanders to protect any and all beguines.[4] There are other recorded instances where nobility helped establish, support, and extend political protection to beguines. Around 1258, Duchess Aléide of Brabant donated some of her land in Lier (near Antwerp) to three women to begin the beguinage of St. Marguerite. While it never numbered more than seventy beguines, St. Marguerite continued in existence until the second half of the twentieth century.

Beguines dedicated their beguinages and chapels to the Blessed Virgin or to a favored saint. Elizabeth of Hungary (1207–1231), while not considered a beguine herself, was a shining example because of her devotion to the poor and to orphans. Also popular were the third-century martyr Catherine of Alexandria, renowned as an educator and philosopher, and Mary Magdalene, known in the early Christian movement as "the apostle to the apostles." Jesus's command to Mary Magdalene—to go forth and tell the world all that she had seen—was appropriated by beguines. The mission of Mary Magdalene was empowering for beguines who felt that they, too, were "testifying to what they had seen."

The establishment of court beguinages freed both established and newly emerging religious communities—such as the Cistercians, Franciscans, and Dominicans—from pastoral and financial responsibility for groups of women aspiring to join their way of

life. By encouraging the growth of self-supporting court beguinages, the pressure to accept women's informal communities
into their orders lessened. And only in the 1400s did the number of women joining court beguinages level off. There were
several reasons for this. Another informal religious movement,
known as "Brothers and Sisters of the Common Life" or "the
Devout," emerged in parts of the Low Countries and western
Germany in the later 1300s. Some women now chose a community of the "Common Life" over the beguines. Also, beguines
who had understood themselves to be "Dominican" were finally
acknowledged by Dominican men, and were thus no longer
counted as beguine communities. And wars and plagues continued to decimate local populations, limiting funds for the construction of new court beguinages.

As we have seen, despite these court beguinages, many
beguines in the Low Countries and northern Europe lived
in smaller groups. Their convents usually were comprised of
anywhere from three to twenty-four women. Many beguines
preferred to live in such smaller groups, which made it easier
to "move on" when new ministry or preaching opportunities
emerged. Elements of daily life in such convents were similar to
life in court beguinages: gathering for prayer and celebration of
mass (but at the local parish church rather than their own chapel
or church), tending to business enterprises to support themselves
and their ministries, and doing household tasks. Court beguinages required more of an individual beguine's time to support
basic operations of the community, which somewhat limited her
available time for—and choice of—ministry. Court beguinages
were usually also supporting large numbers of indigent beguines,
often known as *paupercule begine*, which required a commitment
of the entire women's community.

———

Common sense dictated the process of receiving a new woman into an existing beguine community. Most beguine communities began informally and remained informal. In the 1200s, beguine communities in much of Europe were shaped by the diversity of women who actively participated: wealthy women, poor women, noble women, women newly arrived from the countryside seeking employment in emerging crafts and industries, merchant-class women, widows with children, and elderly women. A common interest in prayer and service in their town or city drew them together; the catalyst was a shared passion for independence, for an intense spiritual life, and for ministry.

Friends invited friends to join their beguine community. Aunts invited nieces. Cousins invited cousins. Rarely were total strangers invited to join—until they were known and had become friends with the beguines. In established beguine communities, a room might become available and an invitation would be extended. Or an outside woman might become aware of an empty room in a beguinage and request admittance. Other women put themselves on a "wait list." Even if a home became available for purchase within a court beguinage, or adjoining land became available for purchase on which a home could be built, the prospective buyer would still need to apply for admittance to the women's community. In convents, the full membership accepted or rejected a woman's request to join them. In larger court beguinages, the council of elders made the final decision concerning acceptance.

A woman would be invited to live with the community on a trial basis—usually for one year—and then there would be a welcoming ceremony within the house. If she fit in and was content with life there, she continued to live on a trial basis with the community for another year or so. After these initial two years, the woman—after her request to become a beguine had

been accepted by the house members or the council of elders—
would be invited to a clothing ceremony, accepting the attire of
a beguine.

The magistra received the promise of a new beguine on behalf
of the entire community of women. The promise was to abide by
the common lifestyle (or rule) of the beguinage and to remain
chastely unmarried while officially a beguine. A second, higher
level of acceptance as a member of the beguinage occurred after
a new beguine had lived there another four years. This particular
acceptance meant that she could be considered for support by, or
admittance to, the infirmary if and when needed.

Medieval nuns wore a unique garb (however, habits were a
nineteenth-century phenomenon) and most beguines, too, did
wear distinctive attire: their clothing was sewn from their own
spun and woven undyed wool, usually of a natural gray or beige
color, and included a hooded cape. Silk gloves, colored stockings,
or decorated sashes were forbidden.

Though a woman promised chastity while living as a beguine,
she remained free to leave the community and marry—medieval
women were very aware of the pressure to marry to preserve
family wealth and lands—and so it was important that a woman's promise of chastity be only for the duration of her life in
the beguine community. On the other hand, a woman could rid
herself of an unwanted husband by entering monastic life. The
church extended this same "approved separation" to married
women entering a beguine community, and thus some beguines
had estranged husbands.

In the earlier 1200s in northern Europe, men were permitted
to enter beguinages to visit relatives and friends. While most
visits occurred during the daytime and in parlors set aside for
guests, there are records of men visiting beguines in their private homes, in private rooms, or in the dormitories. By the later

1200s this practice was restricted to approved parlors, with other women nearby—because beguines had been suffering from accusations of sexual promiscuity and prostitution. To avoid losing their lands and wealth, beguines were forced to take steps to protect their standing and reputation. (Religious laywomen in Italy appear to have exercised this same initial freedom and then later self-protection. However, most of our related historical records of Italy show these women out in ministry and preaching; less is known of their private lives.)

When possible, a new beguine made a donation to the community's common fund for the maintenance of the house (or court beguinage) and its ministries, usually invested in annuities. She was expected to be able to support herself for at least a few years—barring unexpected illness or injury—and to not access the so-called Table of the Holy Spirit, a fund for the poor. In some regions a custom emerged wherein the new beguine, after making her commitment, provided a feast for the beguine community, "not to exceed three courses."

Most beguine communities lived together under a rule of life, which was not a formal legal or church document as was a monastic order's rule. Rather, these beguine rules of life were the living tradition of a particular beguine community that had been formulated by the women themselves. Each community devised its own rule (and wrote it down or memorized it) defining the common aspects of their life together, and this rule could be amended as the women found preferable or necessary. The rule of life clarified the practical aspects of the beguines' shared life and expressed the spirituality, goals, and aspirations of the entire group.

The rule of life defined prayer times and other communal devotional practices. It stipulated prayers on behalf of benefactors and friends, remembrances for the deceased, and practices at the deathbed of friends and family. The rule stated how a beguine community would take care of its infirm and elderly members, the practical concerns involved with a common fund, as well as any common ministry commitments the community might choose to undertake.

The oldest rule of life (that we know of) for the court beguinage *Ten Wijngaard* in Brugge survives in a manuscript written in the late thirteenth or early fourteenth century. In part, this document states that "the beguines of Wyngarde and the people who would like to follow their manner of life will observe the rule of the Apostles: to know the commandments of the Holy Church, and the love of God above all else and the love of neighbor as oneself. They shall keep themselves pure of heart and body, that is to say, of will and acts. And in order that their communal life shall be more spiritual and more peaceful, they shall adopt certain rules, consigned to writing in order that they be more faithfully observed."[5]

Beguine communities were informal and largely nonhierarchical. Most court beguinages held monthly gatherings of the entire community, called chapters, attended by their pastor. Each individual house within the court beguinage gathered on Fridays to discuss business. Individual convents also gathered once weekly to discuss necessary business of concern to them all.

Every beguinage had a chosen leader, a woman known for her wisdom and ability to guide the community. This leader was sometimes called the grand magistra or the grand mistress. The magistra was chosen by her fellow beguines or, in the case of a large court beguinage, the council of elders. She supervised the overall operations and ministries. Most known rules of life stipulated that the magistra was to be merciful, gracious, just, and sympathetic to the women who lived with her—and to be capable of bringing solace to the poor and ill. The council of elders, which consisted of women chosen from among the full membership, advised and aided the magistra in the running of the beguinage and its ministries.

Most medieval nuns in Europe lived under some expression of the Rule of Benedict, a sixth-century set of rules for monastics living in community that became the norm for Western Christian monasticism by the first millennium. Clearly, beguines were influenced by the more moderate expressions of the Benedictine way: choosing a leader who evidenced pastoral concerns, making major life decisions together, and, in larger communities, choosing certain elders to handle day-to-day business decisions. However, beguines were free to choose their leaders without outside interference. As we have seen, nuns were under the scrutiny of the local bishop or abbot, and too often the abbot's or bishop's choices were foisted upon the nuns. They were limited in their income-producing ventures and what ministry they might accomplish behind the monastery walls. Beguines, on the other hand, engaged in business and active ministry and could own private property—nuns could not. Beguines could part ways amicably, while this sort of departure was rare for nuns.

Beguines embraced simplicity but did own property, either individually or as a community. The only requirement within their rule of life was restraint: to live soberly, to avoid displays of wealth, and to share with others what was not essential. Much like the Amish or Shakers in America in later centuries, beguines sought simplicity in the design and furnishing of their homes. They slept on straw mats and developed furniture shaped by the simplicity of lines and multiple uses. They ate healthily but simply, choosing the coarse bread of the poor.

The rule of life would generally stipulate that beguines never go out alone. Whether leaving the beguinage for business, for ministry, for personal matters, or on behalf of the beguinage, beguines had to have a companion. Besides personal safety, this rule was strictly observed to protect the reputation of the beguines. Slander included accusations of sexual promiscuity and prostitution. Beguines were also not to stay away from the beguinage overnight except in an emergency and with permission of the magistra.

Sources of income for the common fund of each house needed to be defined in the rule of life, stating each beguine's responsibility for this common fund. Also clarified was the manner of care for poor and indigent beguines as well as for other poor women. Since most court beguinages and certain convents owned and supported a home for destitute beguines, a secure and steady source of income was needed. Each beguine also contributed to the general fund for the overall running of the beguinage.

Most rules of life also limited the number of beguines who were out attending to the dying: at least two women, and no more than seven, was the general guideline. By the fifteenth and sixteenth centuries, these rules of life—in order to protect beguines from slander—forbade them to keep vigil with the dying except for aristocrats (who were often their benefactors and protectors), the beguines' pastors, or the local bishop. Of course, beguines sat vigil at one another's deathbed.

Separate from the "internal" rule of life were the "external" statutes, proper legal documents filed with the local government. These statutes protected the legal rights and property of the beguinage and stipulated the beguines' relationship and responsibilities toward the secular government. Civic records reveal that beguines were rather sophisticated in their business and political dealings. The use of civil legal documents protected beguine autonomy against interference from families and ecclesiastical authority. Beguines paid civic taxes on their properties, annuities, and other income. Beguines did not claim tax exemption as

monastics always did (even when well-meaning church authorities offered to assist beguines in gaining tax-exempt status).
When the local bishop attempted to convert a beguinage into
church property—which seemed to have happened mostly in
northern Europe and was feared by the beguines since it would
put them under the direct authority of the bishop—the civil
authorities refused to go along due to the potential loss of tax
revenue. The municipalities needed these tax revenues coming
from the beguines. When church authorities tried to suppress
and disband beguinages on suspicion of heresy, or when they
were simply trying to confiscate beguine property, the beguines
found grateful supporters in the local magistrates who supported
the women against legal action. Beguines were comfortable with
such secular legal practices; they wisely established good relations with local civic authorities, registering beguinage statutes
with town or city elders and including them in major decisions.

The rule of life defined procedures when a woman chose to
leave—or was asked to leave—the beguine community. If a
beguine departed the beguinage of her own will, her "entrance
fee" was, for the most part, retained by the house. The rule stipulated how much of the money paid by a woman to the common
fund at her entry would be returned—if any. Many beguines
owned property in their own right, and this remained theirs.
Some beguine rules stipulated that a departing beguine with
significant financial means would make a contribution to the
"poor house," the home beguines owned and sustained for destitute women.

Beguines who owned property bequeathed it in their wills: to
family, to friends, to individual beguines, as well as to their beguinages. Frequently provision was made for the care of the poor.
Beguines who had few possessions left their Psalter (if they were

so fortunate to own one), bedding, clothing, and household utensils to others upon their death. Surviving wills reveal that wealthier beguines also bequeathed money or other incomes for remembering their death anniversary. Sometimes this meant that part of a beguine's estate was to be used to purchase wine, meat, fish, or bread, to be distributed to those in the hospital and to the poor on the deceased's death anniversary or on her favorite feast days. For example, Crise Tsflogheleere, a beguine of St. Alexis in Dendermonde (east of Ghent), in 1471 left her rights to half of a house in the beguinage to any daughter of her brother who expressed a desire to become a beguine—as long as this occurred before the young woman turned fifteen. Shortly thereafter, Christine Coucke, a member of the beguinage St. Elizabeth in Kortrijk, bequeathed her house to her eleven-year-old granddaughter, but only if she became a beguine.[6] (Friends and family, patrons, and other supporters of beguines also made bequests in their wills in the form of property, rents, or cash to support beguines as long as they remained in the beguinage.)

If a beguine left in shame, usually due to an unexpected pregnancy, she forfeited all her belongings. For many beguinages in northern Europe, to expel a beguine usually required consensus of the house. While departure was usually considered permanent, there are some stories of beguine communities that did welcome back a woman who had left "in shame" due to a pregnancy—often she brought the child with her to be raised within the community. The oldest statutes for the beguinage St. Catherine in Mechelen (composed between 1286 and 1300) declared that any beguine found to be pregnant must be removed from the beguine community for at least a year, once her condition became evident. The statutes allowed for the "fallen" beguine's return if her good behavior warranted this.[7] While beguines were sensitive to behavior that compromised their ability to lead independent lives, they also realized that a "disgraced" woman was marginalized by society and had limited opportunities to have a dignified life. By returning to her beguine community and raising her child within the beguinage, a woman was saved from a forced marriage or a life of prostitution.

From their earliest days, beguines were admired by their fellow citizens for being self-supporting. Mendicants—Franciscans and Dominicans—begged alms for their livelihood. Nuns relied upon their dowries, wise investments, and alms to support the monastery. But beguines operated small businesses and engaged in commerce to support themselves and to fund their chosen ministries. It was rare to hear stories of beguines begging for personal support, as they were too aware of the many truly destitute people in towns and cities dependent upon alms for their daily survival. (One exception might have been some of the penitentiae of Italy who begged for alms as an expression of humility.)

Beguines were wise and prudent businesswomen. Not only did they own property and collect rents, they also possessed farms and received rents-in-kind in the form of grain or meat. Legal documents show that the beguines kept close tabs on landholdings and were quite willing to call upon authorities to exercise their legal rights when they felt these were infringed upon. These women were active participants in the property market, buying and selling small and large amounts of land.

Beguines made loans and bought annuities, with the yearly payments serving as income. Some of them made their living in the world of finance: changing money, extending letters of credit, and granting loans. In certain cities that belonged to the Hanseatic League—the powerful merchant association of cities in northern Germany, the Low Countries, Scandinavia, and Britain—beguines were registered merchants.

Beguines were very involved in the textile industry, including purchasing and processing sheep's fleece, spinning, dyeing, and weaving the fine woven wool for which the Low Countries and northern Italy became famous. Beguines hackled, combed, and spun wool, napped and finished woven woolen cloth, prepared it for dyeing, and also cut and prepared flax for the production of linens. Beguines worked as tailors and embroiderers, also taking in small jobs of sewing and washing laundry. And they trained the unskilled to work in some aspects of the textile production.

After the heavy loom had been introduced in the twelfth century, increasing the productivity of the weavers, the demand for women to prepare the wool and finish the cloth grew. Beguines would gather for work parties, and the Psalter or other religious texts would be read and discussed while they worked. They also employed other beguines, supplying them with raw materials and trading the finished product on the local market.

Records show that beguines in Aalst (near Brussels), Antwerp, Bergues (near Calais), Brugge, Diest, Herentals (near Antwerp), Maastricht, Mechelen, and Tongeren were weaving and trading cloth in the thirteenth and fourteenth centuries, thus working in direct competition with the powerful guilds. The keen business skills of many beguines could cause them trouble with competitors such as the guilds, and even led to open hostility. Beguines, like women in general, were not supposed to compete with men or better them in the public realm. In the Low Countries and elsewhere in northern Europe, guilds felt threatened by the beguines' willingness to work for less income and by their ability to produce cloth at lower prices than guild artisans. Laws were variously enacted that applied only to beguines and restricted their income and limited their cloth output—all due to political pressure from the guilds that were unable to compete effectively with the beguines. Eventually, laws were passed in different parts of Europe that limited the use of spindles by beguines; any beguine found to have violated this restriction was fined, and any cloth produced by beguines beyond the assigned quantity was given to the poor. In Strasbourg, for example, in the early 1300s, the use of the spinning wheel was prohibited for the beguines due to guild pressure. A similar prohibition happened in Cologne in 1375. In the later 1400s, the local guilds of silk spinners declared that giving work to beguines was grounds for expulsion.

The bizzoche and penitentiae of northern Italy were also involved in all stages of cloth production—but they did not encounter the challenges of powerful guilds, as did the beguines north of the Alps. Laws were not enacted against the trades of these Italian women, and they developed a distinctive cloth for the poor that came to be known as *panni humiliati*.

Beguinages endured the ravages of war and plague, hostile politics and shifting cultural attitudes. Yet some beguine communities, through sheer strength of leadership, determined membership, and creative thinking, managed to survive all the way into the twentieth century. One example is the court beguinage St. Elizabeth in Kortrijk, which had been established around 1240. Through the gracious actions of Countess Joan, St. Elizabeth added buildings over the years, and its chapel was completed in 1284. Then it survived near total destruction by warring troops in 1302.

The beguines rebuilt St. Elizabeth in 1315 and operated a hospital there by 1349. During the Battle of Westrozebeke in 1382, Breton mercenaries plundered and damaged the beguinage. Yet between 1425 and 1450, at least fifty-two women joined St. Elizabeth, and by 1464 the chapel had been rebuilt. The beguinage's oldest surviving statutes, written by its magistra Marie vanden Brande, date to the year 1440.

In 1572 and again in 1578, the beguinage suffered damage at the hands of Calvinist troops. The beguines were driven away and their homes occupied by soldiers. But a few years later, the women were able to resume their life at the beguinage. Young women joined, and by 1612 the complex was enlarged yet again. More than 140 beguines were living there by the 1630s.

In 1684 the French seized Kortrijk, and most of the beguinage was burned down. For many years the surviving beguines were heavily taxed by the French but managed to continue their lifestyle. Still deemed a threat to the power and wealth of the guilds, the beguines of Kortrijk were prohibited from dealing in lace, linen, or other goods under penalty of confiscation and expulsion from their beguinage.

During the French Revolution the beguines were in fact expelled from their home, but in 1801, when Sophia Decruenaere was elected magistra, she regained the right for beguines to live in St. Elizabeth and wear their traditional beguine attire. Then the Secularization took place, but in 1846 the French government "rented" a portion of the beguinage back to the beguines. The magistra at the time, Maria-Joanna Maertens, attempted to retrieve the remainder of their complex from the government. The last formal magistra of St. Elizabeth was Clementia Hiers (1819–1899). The complex was severely damaged during the First World War, but an attempt at continued beguine life emerged with Laura Deconick (who died in 1990) and Marcella Pattyn. The long and varied history of the beguinage St. Elizabeth drew to a close with the passing of Marcella Pattyn in 2013.

Beguines across Europe showed creative determination to survive over the centuries. More than we may comprehend, these women were unified in their commitment to ministry. Their independent lifestyle was a tool to work with the marginalized and the poor, in ways that they personally chose—and not under the direction and control of a bishop or nobleman. Their ministry was an expression of God's love for all, a love the beguines sought to embody. Hadewijch, who lived in the 1200s, wrote in a letter of spiritual direction to a young beguine: "I urge you again and again to practice true love and to aspire to truth and perfection, that you may satisfy God, please Him [God], and do Him honor and justice, first in Himself [God's Presence] and then in the good people He loves and who love Him, and may you give them all they need whatever their state may be. This I urge you to do unceasingly, and this I have done since I came among you, for it is the best and most becoming way to serve God."[8]

4

BEGUINE
MINISTRIES

EGUINES WERE HIGHLY MOTIVATED in their business pursuits by their passion for ministry. In order to conduct the ministries for which they felt a calling, and to minimize outside interference in those chosen ministries, beguines needed independent financing. Scandalized by a lax church leadership seemingly unconcerned with the spiritual well-being of the laity, beguines considered preaching and teaching Scriptures and spiritual formation—alongside aiding the poor and sick—their first and foremost ministries. They yearned to embody the message of Jesus Christ as they understood it: preaching and teaching about God's love for all people. And in imitating Jesus and his early followers, beguines fed the hungry, gave drink to the thirsty, clothed the naked, sheltered the homeless, visited the sick and imprisoned, and buried the dead. Yet these women moved beyond the more "traditional" ministries of adherents to the vita apostolica by establishing and funding infirmaries, educating children, and teaching skills to the poor so that they might care for themselves and their families.

From their earliest days, beguines across Europe visited the sick in their homes, frequently bringing food and providing basic sanitation and health care. They prayed with the invalid and read Scriptures and prayers by their bedside, with the thoughtful intention of wanting to identify with the suffering Christ as expressed in the sick. Beguines pooled their resources to purchase medicines and to learn basic medical practices from the healers in their area. As the demand for their assistance and healing services grew, beguines might have purchased a small piece of land and built a place to care for the sick and destitute: their infirmaries. These infirmaries were an interesting mixture of medical care, prayerful presence, and support for the dying, as well as a safe place for the destitute. Jacques de Vitry was so impressed with the beguine infirmaries he had visited in the Low Countries that he described them (in his *Historia Occidentalis*) as "hospices of piety, houses of honesty, workshops of holiness, convents of the right and devout life, refuges of the poor, sustenance to the wretched, consolation to those in mourning, refectories for the hungry, comfort and relief for those who are ill."[1] These places of healing seem to have been major centers of ministry and hope, often serving both as infirmary and as shelter for the poor.

Beguines received medical training (as much as any was available) in nursing and midwifery from doctors or midwives, or from fellow beguines. Local officials looked to the beguines to provide competent nursing care, acknowledging the beguines' expertise in caring for the sick. Beguines also operated foundling hospitals for orphaned or abandoned babies. And they were often called out for overnight emergencies. These visits to the homes of the seriously ill (or dying) allowed beguines to attempt to ease the patients' pain and to comfort them—and also to pray for their souls as they passed from this world to the next.

Around 1350 in northern France and the Low Countries, some groups of beguines picked up the nickname *Soeurs Grises* (Gray Sisters) because of their garb. They were known for their compassionate care of the sick, nursing them both in the patients' homes and in infirmaries. By 1388, the Gray Sisters were affiliating loosely with Franciscan friars. In 1483, the independent communities of Gray Sisters gathered and created for themselves a set of statutes. Their statutes are the earliest surviving example of women in Europe explicitly proclaiming an active ministry as sanctifying—growing in holiness—in its own right, as opposed to contemplative prayer being the only avenue for sanctification.

The statutes of the Gray Sisters permitted the women to go to the sick when called (to avoid gossip, the Gray Sisters went in pairs), to stay in the sick person's home overnight, and also excused them from attending the Divine Office in order to care for the sick. This last point was considered rather radical at the time—these women were announcing that ministry was as important as attendance at prayer. The Gray Sisters understood that anyone could grow in holiness by attending to the ailing.

Many beguine convents and court beguinages formed around preexisting infirmaries in which the women were working. Frequently beguines expanded their infirmaries as part of the court beguinage complex under construction. Early groups of beguines, including the groups that had formed around Juetta of Huy, Marie d'Oignies, Ida of Nivelles, and Ida of Louvain, cared for both women and men. Due to politically motivated accusations of scandalous behavior, beguines eventually found it necessary to limit their health care to women only (but sometimes they would continue to care for men anyway).

Lepers were true outcasts in medieval society, as they were outlawed from entering towns and cities. A leper's only option for support was begging alms outside the gates and walls. The church had managed, however, to extend a certain degree of protection to lepers. Under Pope Alexander III, the Third Lateran Council's Decree on Lepers (1179)—while regarding leprosy as the product of sin and especially sexual aberration—protected the rights of lepers to gather and form communities for mutual support and protection, to have their own chaplain and cemetery, and to be left alone.

Medical care was virtually nonexistent for lepers unless provided by beguines—they associated themselves with lepers by living with them, caring for them, praying with them. Beguines embraced the church's Decree on Lepers by purchasing land out in the countryside in order to establish hospices known as *leprosaria*, and they created intentional communities of lepers and beguines, building clusters of simple huts around a hospice with a modest chapel for prayer. This beguine commitment was expressed early on by Marie d'Oignies who, as mentioned, was part of a leper-beguine community at Willambroux.

Beguines were believed to straddle the border between life and death in a powerful way and so could help the dying in their final days, easing their path to heaven. Attending to the dying and the dead was a ministry rooted in the beguines' compassion and love for others. Over time they became so identified with their ministry of caring for, and sitting with, the dying that they became known as "funeral specialists."

Beguines were frequently called to the homes of the dying in order to pray with them and read Scripture aloud, and they also performed this service for the many poor who lay dying in the beguine infirmaries. As was common practice in medieval times, beguines prayed the Psalter of the Virgin (the Liturgy of the Hours with a focus on Marian texts). This Psalter often included the Seven Penitential Psalms, hymns dedicated to Mary, and the Office of the Dead, which allowed a diversity of possible prayers to meet the beguines' own devotional needs or the needs of the people to whom they were attending.

After a person had died, the beguines washed the body, preparing it for the so-called laying out—the vigil before the funeral when family and friends could sit with the deceased. Beguines also stayed with the deceased through the funeral until burial.

Since medieval society was deeply concerned about the transition from this world into the next, people with some financial means would leave specific instructions in their will for their own death watch, funeral, and burial. Money would be left to beguinages with the stipulation that a certain number of beguines would sit with the donor as that person lay dying, praying for their salvation, staying with them for the funeral procession and mass, and accompanying the deceased to the graveside. Medieval people were understandably afraid of the process of dying and the "crossing over" and believed that the presence of beguines would ease this process and possibly even ensure a quick entrance into heaven.

Originally, beguines attended to anyone who had requested their presence while dying. By the fourteenth century, accusations of impropriety—beguines were accused of socializing and cavorting with men under the guise of sitting with the dying—had increased. (As we have seen, beguines across Europe had to live with accusations of sexual immorality because their accusers assumed independent women would always be immoral.) Beguines mitigated these accusations by no longer going alone to the dying, but soon it was necessary to go in groups of several beguines and to attend only to dying women (unless a man on his deathbed was a close relative or honorable cleric). On the other hand, beguines were free to attend to the dying in the beguinages' infirmaries.

Medieval wills reveal much about the personal devotions of people and the particular care and attention paid to their final hours and death. Frequently a person's instructions for their last days, their funeral, and the annual remembrances were detailed with great care. These remembrances were called chantries or *memoria*. Chantries were endowments for the celebration of masses and saying prayers in honor of a deceased person or a family. A side altar or chapel within a large church might also be endowed by a chantry and dedicated to a particular person or family, who was usually wealthy. Since beguines could not preside at mass, they hired priests to celebrate the memorial masses at the beguines' instructions. In larger cities, beguinages were managing so many memoria bequeathed to them in wills that beguinages might hire a priest solely to celebrate such chantry masses.

The wills often stipulated which prayers would be said for the dead until their burial, and they provided the money for a certain number of candles to be burned in remembrance of the deceased. Sometimes the candles were to be burned during the month immediately after the death, and sometimes on the anniversary of the death until the money ran out. A similar practice existed for specified prayers on the anniversary of deaths.

There are hundreds of examples where people left rents, property, and money to beguine communities large and small to celebrate offices or offer masses for the benefit of their souls, usually on the anniversary of their death, the feast day of their patron saint, or another favorite saint's day. For example, in the 1260s, Ghillain de Saint Venant donated the rental income on two houses she owned in Douai to a community of beguines to pay for an obituary mass for her soul to be celebrated each year on the anniversary of her death.[2] Bernard Pilates, also in the thirteenth century, decreed that the ten beguines in the convent he founded in Douai were to recite five Our Fathers and five Hail Marys before an image of the Virgin each day.[3] Peter of Taviers, chaplain at the cathedral of St. Lambert in Liège, left funds in his will of 1291 to buy a house for twelve beguines in a local parish, requesting that they pray the vigils of the Office of the Dead and the Seven Penitential Psalms for the salvation of his soul.[4]

But memoria administered by beguines were often also of a material sort. A family might donate money or rent income and, in return, beguines would provide beer and bread to the poor on the death anniversary of the person being remembered. For example, the widow Elzebe Raesfeldt of Bocholt (in northwest Germany) established a memoria in 1509, and a portion of her gift was to be used to bake bread five times a year in honor of the five wounds of Christ. This bread was to be handed out on the evenings of the four major yearly feasts (Christmas, Easter, Assumption, and Pentecost) as well as on Michaelmas. Loaves were to be baked and handed out to the oldest and poorest thirteen people in Bocholt as well as to three schoolchildren diligent about learning. The magistra was to use some of the money to include butter or meat with the bread. The days Raesfeldt had chosen for her memoria reflected the lay belief that the spiritual power of these holy days was so great because the veil between heaven and earth was thinner then and thus prayers more efficacious.[5]

These memoria funds and the care beguines extended to the dying were causing problems—priests responsible for the financial oversight of their parishes were losing money to these women. Traditionally, death fees were paid to parishes upon the passing of a family member. Increasingly, these fees were paid to the beguines who were doing the burying, and consequently the animosity toward beguines by parish priests and bishops grew. This simmering conflict was addressed in 1303 when Pope Boniface VIII ordered beguines to turn over one quarter of the death fee to the parish of the decedent's birth.

All matters pertaining to the afterlife carried an economic factor: chantries/memoria and death fees, which were believed to have a direct effect upon a person's salvation, were a profitable source of income and an integral part of the local economy.

In medieval Europe prostitutes, like lepers, had to wear distinctive clothing. This clothing exposed them to sexual assault and made leaving prostitution difficult—both socially and economically. Beguines worked with women trying to get out of prostitution, giving them a new place to stay (among beguines) to begin a new life and providing them with the skills and means to support themselves. Too many daughters from poor families were regularly sold onto the street by their families. While some beguines went out into the streets to save these young women, most of them were rescued from prostitution by clerics and other men (usually followers of the vita apostolica) who brought them to the beguines for help. With their network of homes and contacts, beguines could slip prostitutes out of town to safer places where they were not known and could begin anew with a "clean" reputation. Some of the infirmaries that beguines ran also offered shelter to such stigmatized women. But many people condemned the willingness of beguines to shelter and work with prostitutes, and once more beguines faced suspicions of sexual immorality.

Beguines also cared for escaped slaves. While serfs were understood to be an extension of the land that they were legally tied to, thus making serfs the "property" of the landowner, slavery was the buying and selling of people independent of land. Slavery in the Middle Ages was mostly the result of conquerors selling the conquered people to traders to be taken to the Byzantine Empire and further eastward. Girls were also sold to brothels across Europe. While the church condemned and prohibited slavery, it continued anyway. Beguines provided a safe haven for escaped slaves, especially women and children.

The great seaport of Venice was one of the hubs of this slave trade. Like the beguines of northern Europe, religious laywomen in Venice were from all social classes and worked with the marginalized of every background. In the early sixteenth century, these women were sponsoring homes for orphan girls and reformed prostitutes. By the 1540s, Paola Antonia Negri[6] and her fellow pinzochere traversed Venice attending to hospitals and informal communities for women that they had established and managed. Negri's ministry ignited fierce controversy and she was eventually forced to enter an enclosed monastery. According to her chief accuser, Negri's work was deemed inappropriate for a mere woman.

A few decades later in Venice, Adriana Contarini and Helena Priuli brought together a group of financially independent women and established a safe home for young girls who had been sold into prostitution. Contarini and Priuli established legal documents of protection and wrote a rule for their house, known as *Le Constituzioni et Regole della Casa delle Cittelle di Venetia*. In a letter, Adriana Contarini wrote: "We have succeeded in sheltering thirty little girls, all snatched from the power of the devil; we see the degradation of these girl-children who, at the age of twelve or thirteen or even younger, have been sold by their own mothers; they come from all social ranks, from the nobility, the middle class, the workers. Our times are so disastrous, that no words can express the wretchedness of some of the cases."[7] This group of women expanded their home, moved several times in search of safer locations for the children, and built a chapel, Santa Maria della Presentazione, which was consecrated in 1588.

Beguines emerged at a time of renewed literacy. While very few people could read Latin—the ultimate standard of literacy—the twelfth and thirteenth centuries witnessed an increase in the education of children. Both nobility and common people recognized the practical value of education, even for their daughters, as a boon to the economy.

As we have seen, beguines made their own initial and ongoing education a priority. At the foundation of the court beguinage of Champfleury in Douai in 1245, the beguines secured a commitment by the collegiate chapter of St. Amé of Douai to appoint a competent cleric to give instruction to the women at the beguinage in the "learned disciplines." There and elsewhere, beguines bargained with monks, clerics, and other teachers for access to learning in order to advance their knowledge.

Many future beguines were educated by beguines (some of whom were recluses) who provided instruction and guidance to girls. The young Ida of Nivelles, Beatrijs of Nazareth, and Ida of Gorsleeuw were all cared for and instructed by anonymous recluses. Juetta of Huy, after she had become a recluse, raised at least three girls.

Thus beguines were well-known, even revered, as educators. They taught children reading and writing, decorum and manners, morals and music. Sometimes Latin and another foreign language would be included, especially for the gifted students. Beguines taught the Bible, prayer and devotions, and sometimes theology. By the 1270s, some beguines were using their own informal Bible translations and commentaries in the vernacular for religious instruction, despite the perception of many theologians and clerics that any woman translating the Bible into the vernacular was radical and therefore must be condemned.

Children were a common sight around beguinages. While some were orphans being raised by the beguine community, most children either came from nearby for daily education or were boarders attending the beguine school. While most beguine communities educated a small number of children at a time, some court beguinages, including those in Avesnes (northern France), Herentals, Kortrijk, and Diest, by the 1400s and 1500s[8] were educating so many children that they needed to build special schoolhouses to provide sufficient space.

Certain court beguinages included a *schola* or special music school to teach children elementary Latin and chant for choir service. Music, both sacred as well as popular, was important to beguines. While beguines were known to sing for enjoyment while working together, they also valued well-executed chant and sacred singing for mass and other prayer services.

Above all, beguines were compassionate toward the many (urban) poor. Beggars constantly came to their doors and gates seeking help. Beguines provided clothing and shoes, food and guidance. At nightfall the poor could slip in through the gates of the court beguinages and sleep undisturbed in the courtyard.

The large number of truly destitute poor was a phenomenon emerging with the rise of urbanization. Before the advent of medieval cities, the poor lived in the villages where they were known and where farmers and craftsmen could feed another person. In cities, the poor were separated from the rural support structure and from what kin they might have had. In order to combat urban poverty, the so-called Table of the Holy Ghost was developed in the thirteenth century in urban parishes in northern

Europe. This was a fund—of coins and food items—administered by trusted individuals in the parish to support hospitals and the poor. Beguines also ran Tables of the Holy Ghost within beguinages; funds were collected among beguines and their friends and administered by the elders of the beguine community.

In 1284, the beguines of St. Elizabeth of Ghent wrote to their major benefactor, Count Guy Dampierre (a son of Countess Margaret), and told him that their court beguinage had established a Table of the Holy Spirit (Holy Ghost) to support the beguinage's elderly poor—estimated to be around three hundred women—after they had realized that these poor in their midst had eaten only bread for a long time.[9] Surviving wills reveal a common practice of beguines and their friends providing annuities, paid yearly, to benefit the Table of the Holy Ghost. Those responsible for the Table coordinated the distribution of rye, bread, fish, oil, cloth, and shoes to the impoverished.

Because beguines cared for both indigent beguines and elderly women, most court beguinages included one or more separate homes available for these women. And when the booming textile industry in the Low Countries attracted single women from the countryside into the cities, beguines purchased additional homes to provide safe havens and moral support for these women who were alone and vulnerable. Since beguines taught indigent women marketable skills to develop a trade or business so that they could become self-supporting, and because so many beguines were involved in the cloth trade, many indigent women could learn from and work with beguines in this trade.

In Spain, the beatas also owned homes to offer a haven for destitute women. As a number of men left Spain in the 1500s to colonize the Americas, more women were left to fend for themselves and their children. But Spanish society rejected a public role for women. Beatas negotiated a middle way, creating the means for women to support themselves without being threatened or harmed. They were also extensively involved in ministry to women in prison. The population of female prisoners had grown alarmingly large due to poverty, allegations of heresy (usually "guilt by association"), and prostitution. Beatas visited female prisoners and aided in their release whenever feasible.

The ministry of beguines was driven and nourished by their inner life of spirituality. Their profound experience of the divine presence impelled them to serve the hurting and defenseless around them; and their dedication in ministry enriched their prayer life. Ministry and spirituality were threads that wove the same cloth. The great beguine mystic Marguerite Porete declared that "kindness toward others obeys no created thing but Love. Kindness toward others possesses nothing of her own, and if she does possess something, she never says it belongs to her. Kindness toward others skips her own needs to help a neighbor [. . .] kindness toward others gives to her neighbors all she has that's worth anything. She keeps nothing for herself. Her amazing generosity often makes her promise what she doesn't have because she knows the more she gives, the more she receives in her soul. Kindness toward others is such a wise businesswoman that she earns profits everywhere when others go out of business."[10] And Mechthild of Magdeburg said that the day of her spiritual awakening was the day she saw—and knew she saw—all things in God and God in all things.

5
༃

BEGUINE
SPIRITUALITY

OU ARE TIME-TRAVELING once more to the medieval court beguinage in Flanders. Again you are greeted at the gate by one of the older beguines. Once inside, you see families who must have been spending the night in the spacious courtyard, safe from marauding gangs. Children are chasing chickens and geese, and laundry is drying on lower tree branches. Some of these families might head back to the countryside now that the busy market days are over. You approach the beguine's home you had visited before and hear the laughter of children inside: your host and her fellow beguines have taken in three orphaned girls, plucked off the wharf and saved from the brothels to be educated and trained in cloth finishing.

After a boisterous meal of lamb and vegetables in honor of Eastertide, you all leave for the beguinage's church. Other beguines, many accompanied by children, and even a few men, are joining you there. To your surprise, the bell begins to toll. In parish churches, one only hears the tolling of bells for High Mass and significant events like the death of a ruler.

Inside their church, the beguines carry the wooden chairs and desks toward the walls, thus clearing a large space for easy movement. Some elderly beguines sit down on the chairs along the walls; other beguines set up and tune musical instruments.

The music and singing commences; the songs are lively and familiar. You happily join in. The beguines are clapping to the beat of the music and begin a gentle swaying movement. With the third song, you all enter into an informal, gentle dance, moving first toward the left and then toward the right. Feet stamp and hands sway in rhythm to the music. Soon beguines are weaving around one another in a style echoing folk dances. The church is filled with harmonious sound and movement. The children, who had shared in the dancing, at some point tucker out and rest for a while near the elders.

The beguine community enters into song after song—songs of poetic aspiration and Scripture. The church interior is warm; skin glows. Eventually the activities quiet down and the beguines stand or sit in silence. Some of the elders light candles. The magistra of the beguinage climbs the steps to the pulpit and there seems to be a divine energy flowing among the beguines. Your host excitedly whispers that their leader speaks through the inspiration of the Holy Spirit. Into the silence the magistra begins:

"If you want faith, pray. If you want hope, pray. If you want kindness, pray. If you want poverty, pray. If you want obedience, pray. If you want integrity, pray. If you want humility, pray. If you want gentleness, pray. If you want strength, pray. If you want any virtue, pray.

Like this: Always read the Book of Life, which is the life of the God-Man, Jesus Christ, who lived in poverty, pain, scorn, and true obedience. Do not skim this book. Let it penetrate you while you read it. It will teach you everything you need to know, no matter your present circumstances. It will fill you with a burning fire that will be your greatest consolation.

And the more you pray, the more you will be enlightened. As you pray, you will see God's goodness more deeply. And the deeper and more excellent your spiritual eyesight, the more you will love. The more you love, the more joy you will take in all you see, and the greater your joy, the greater your understanding. Then you will reach the completeness of Light because you will understand you cannot understand anything at all."[1]

The magistra continues preaching for some time, exhorting her listeners to a deeper love for God and to compassion for the poor and unfortunate. At last she steps down from the pulpit.

There is intense silence, until quiet weeping by a few beguines can be heard. Others begin to sing. The magistra slowly moves among the praying and singing beguines. She stops here and there and lays her hands on one of the women, praying softly. Someone calls out, asking the magistra to pray for her. And then another beguine beckons for prayer. At last the instruments are picked up, and the beguines begin to dance again, filling their beautiful church with joy.

The expressive prayer of beguines of northern Europe and beatas of Spain was as profound as that experienced centuries later among American Quakers, Shakers, and other religious groups. Both these medieval women and American religious groups, under what they felt was the powerful sway of the Holy Spirit, were willing to give expression outwardly to what they experienced inwardly. Each embodied their deepest prayerful adoration with tears, laughter, dancing, and "being slain in the Spirit" (a person drops to the ground in intense silence).

The inner spiritual world of the beguines was rich in imagination. These women, and some of their monastic contemporaries, instigated a seismic shift in the province of the imagination, bringing their embodied experience of God and their spiritual journey into a broadened and deepened inner realm. Beguine mystics experienced a fiercely intimate encounter with the Divine—whom they called both "God" and "the One"—to the point that the term "mystical consciousness" might be more accurate than "mystical experience." Mystics have insisted that their experiences are more than mere unusual sensations, but rather comprise new ways of knowing and loving based on a heightened awareness of the Divine as the direct and transforming center of their lives.

Beguines were heavily involved in the development and promotion of what we now call "incarnational piety" and "affective devotion."[2] They *embodied* their prayer and devotion, seeking to emotionally enter into their experience of prayer. These were private dramas of their hearts. While the medieval church in general focused its devotion and preaching on the crucified Christ, beguines were especially devoted to the earthly human Jesus. They were renowned for this devotion to the humanity of Jesus and to the events of his earthly life. Beguines would meditate on certain gospel stories, in their imaginations reliving the story by "placing" themselves at gospel scenes such as Jesus's birth; the adolescent Jesus in the Temple; his preaching missions; and, particularly, "journeying with" Jesus through his betrayal, trial, scourging, and Crucifixion. Where medieval theologians crafted intellectual treatises on the presence of Christ, beguines sought and reportedly received physical experiences of the Christ they knew as present in their midst. Douceline of Digne, for example, instructed her followers to feel and weep for the Passion of Christ. "For all Christians," she said, "have a great duty to remember the passion of the Lord, at least once a day. For we must never forget this blessing, but continually carry in our hearts the death of Christ, for which we live as widows, with our heads covered."[3] Beguines did not want merely to commemorate the Crucifixion; they aspired to embody the experience, wanted to feel what it might have felt like for Jesus to be crucified.

Beguines "placed" themselves into this event, often while praying also holding devotional images such as a carved pietà, a "Man of Sorrows" (a painted image of Christ gazing at the viewer and showing his wounds), or a crucifix, thereby seeking to feel what Jesus might have experienced and embodying their prayer. A wracking emotional response was commonly reported, along with a deep sense of expanded love and compassion. Marie d'Oignies embraced the feet of a carved crucifix in passionate prayer. On another occasion she reported that rays of light had emanated from the cross and pierced her heart. In Liège, the recluse Eve of Saint Martin (c. 1210–after 1264) prayed while holding a so-called Veronica, which was a cloth onto which an image of the crucified Christ was painted—in reference to the merciful woman in the Passion story who wiped the brow of Jesus as he was being led to Calvary. Veronica clothes were common among beguines. One time, after praying with her Veronica, Eva showed it to her teacher and mentor, Juliana of Mont-Cornillon, who reportedly responded by feeling the pain of Christ's Passion and then fainted.

Ida of Louvain (c. 1212–c. 1275) was said to have "bathed the baby Jesus" while in prayer. Numerous beguines spoke of seeing the infant Jesus while gazing at the eucharist—raised high for all to see—at mass. Some beguines prayed with a so-called liturgical cradle, which was an infant's cradle in which a figure of the Christ-child could be placed. Beguines apparently then rocked this cradle while they prayed, thus "comforting the infant Jesus."[4] Such bodily and sensual responses in prayer and to objects of devotion were not considered extraordinary or unusual by any means in medieval times.

Juliana of Mont-Cornillon, also in the 1200s, deeply embraced the stages of Jesus's life, and "on the feast of the Lord's Annunciation her emotional year began. With devout and loving footsteps, she followed every saving deed that Christ enacted in the flesh and the holy Church remembers, and thus she wondrously passed through the cycle of the liturgical year. On the Lord's Annunciation, the first festival, she sensed great joy and comfort in the angel's address to Mary and in the modest but wise Virgin's response. For just as Christ endowed her with marvelous knowledge and love when she considered the Sacrament of his Body and Blood, so also the Virgin Mary compassionately illumined her with the fire of love and the light of understanding when she contemplated the Lord's Incarnation."[5] We can trust that this devotion was very real and personal for Juliana. And something else was happening: she was teaching her followers the sacred stories around the earthly life of Jesus along with some rather sophisticated theology.

In their embodied prayer, many beguines swooned on the cross with Jesus Christ himself—not as passive observers but sharing in the terror of the Crucifixion; other beguines became enraptured with Mary standing before the cross. Lutgard of Aywières, a contemporary of Juliana, was reportedly observed levitating while she was in prayer, light emanating from her and oil dripping miraculously from her fingers and with a mystical crown on her head. Douceline of Digne, while in rapturous prayer, was found "weeping in anguish for the sorrow of the Virgin and her son. She cried loudly, in such bitter grief that it pained them all to hear her so distraught. Her cries could be heard from a great distance. She had such compassion for the Virgin and was so filled with grief that it seemed as if she must die with her. It was evident from all the signs she showed and from her great sorrow that the suffering which Jesus Christ endured had been revealed to her. She felt it so strongly that it seemed as if every vein in her body was going to burst from the pain caused by what she had seen."[6]

Through their close imitation of Christ's life, and by cherishing the bodiliness of both Jesus and Mary, beguines were elevating the human body in general. Women gave birth, women nursed babies, women prepared food for the family, and women cared for the sick and dying. To beguines, Jesus as "God-man" affirmed the worthiness of humanity in all its flesh-ness and ordinariness: every human person was capable of redemption, including women and outcasts of society such as lepers, prostitutes, and slaves. Beguines were deeply devoted to the Christian concept of the Incarnation—the belief that God had become human in Jesus of Nazareth—and it was an affective experience for them and not merely an intellectual understanding.

Beguine immersion in the gospel story created a medieval "literature of compassion" that scholars define as literature that encourages "suffering with" the Virgin Mary and Jesus Christ, along with emotional participation in the drama of Christ's Passion. Beguines sought to elicit a compassionate response within themselves and among their followers. Importantly, their deep identification with Christ's Passion did not lead them to an experience of victimhood that would have entrapped them in a cycle of self-hatred, self-denigration, or passivity; instead, this kind of immersion resulted in a sense of empowerment for the beguines in a society that allowed women little power. By sharing an embodied experience of the human Jesus, beguines created a communal body of experience (and literature) that transcended the rift of centuries between their own lives and the lifetime of Jesus.

For these women, prayer was being in the presence of God, seeking to unite their minds and hearts with the One they loved (and whom they frequently referred to as their "Beloved"). A central goal in life for beguines was unity of will—that their personal will would become so united with the will of God that they essentially functioned as a unified whole. God's heart would be the seeker's heart; the seeker's heart would find a home in God and God alone. This unity of will would be evidenced by joy, mercy and compassion, and love.

"It is in prayer that one finds God"—so taught Angela of Foligno. Beguines framed their daily lives around prayer. Rising at dawn, they attended mass, either at their local parish church or (if they had one) in their own chapel or church. They also met morning and evening either in their homes or in a chapel for common prayer, using an informal compendium of prayers that each beguinage created and collated, rather than the more traditional liturgy of the monasteries or clergy. Beguine Psalters were usually a combination of prayers dedicated to Mary: the Ave Maria, *Credo in Deum, Confiteor, Miserere mei Deus*, and assorted benedictions. Prayers and poetry that beguines had written themselves were also included in their devotional services. Some beguine communities had additional times of prayer and/or "sacred reading" (of their favorite homilies or writings of theologians), often alongside doing their handiwork. Private prayer included a commitment to praying the Our Father and Hail Mary seven times daily. These prayers were easily memorized and gave each woman a sense of connection with fellow beguines and other friends who were also praying these ancient prayers. They also had dedicated times of silence from after the evening meal until morning.

Both in their prayers and in their daily routines, beguines were deeply devoted to Mary, "Our Lady." Early in the Christian movement, Mary had been given the title *Theotokos*, meaning Mother of God or God-Bearer. As the mother of Jesus, she "birthed the Incarnation, God present in our midst." These were powerful theological statements in a society that was so misogynistic toward women. Mary as "Mother of God" gave women a legitimate place in society and, more importantly, in salvation history, and beguines were sophisticated and adept at using these concepts.

Beguines could relate to Mary, who was seen as the exemplar of beguine life. She had experienced a woman's joys and challenges: raising a child, tending to the needs of an extended family, and living in a violent world. Mary had been a woman in a society that did not respect or protect women; and most importantly, she had watched her son suffer and die.

Thomas of Cantimpré recounted one of the visions that Margaret of Ypres (1216–1237) had of Mary, stating that "the most blessed Virgin Mary appeared to her [Margaret] and, as it seemed to her in spirit, the Venerable Lady placed a hand on Margaret's breast and asked if this was the place of the sorrow and evil by which she was burdened. She replied, 'Yes, my Lady'. And the blessed Virgin asked, 'What is the cause of such languor and grief?' She answered, 'because I have offended you and your Son by so many disgraceful sins.' Without delay the Blessed Mother approached at once, drawing near as if to a fellow sufferer, and drew her hand through her [Margaret's] entire heart and breast, saying these exact words which I shall write: 'I heal you in soul and body. Know that all your sins have been forgiven you by my Son.' Truly blessed and most worthy is she whom the glorious Virgin Mary has deigned to visit and heal from all sorrow!"[7] Such visions revealed a respectful "friendship" with Mary, a great saint whom the beguines perceived as being approachable. Since they were not infrequently mothers or grandmothers themselves, beguines felt a natural affinity for the nurturing and suffering Mother of God. Medieval women sensed that Mary would hear their prayer petitions in a way that an all-male divinity might not. Mary was "real," an earthly friend as well as an effective advocate.

Beguines exhorted their followers to recognize that there existed no impediment to a deep and meaningful prayer life. No matter what a person's station in life, be they educated or uneducated, poor or wealthy, it did not impede or deny them awareness of God in their lives. God yearned to draw close to all. In a society ruled by kings and dukes and lords who kept the majority of people oppressed, and in a church that taught that bishops and priests decided who merited heaven, beguines had some radical things to say. They taught that ordinary people could experience direct intimacy with God without a cleric to advocate on their behalf—no intermediary was required.

Angela of Foligno believed that a loving relationship with God in prayer was not the exclusive domain of the professionally religious but available for all—and then went on to describe in her *Instructions* what this inner journey might be like.

Angela lived in Foligno, an Umbrian town near Assisi. Rich and beautiful, spirited and quick-witted, Angela was married with children. In about 1285, when she was in her later thirties, she underwent a dramatic conversion. Then, after her husband and children had died, she focused her daily life on prayer, fasting, poverty, and serving the poor. She gave away her wealth, became a Franciscan tertiary, and belonged to a group of Franciscans (both lay followers and religious) in her hometown. Even beyond her group of followers she was considered a magistra.

Angela's relationship with the Divine was extraordinary, and some of her behavior frightened others. She would publicly weep for her sins, agonize over a lost sense of God's presence, strip away some of her clothing to express solidarity with Christ's poverty, and "place" herself into Christ's Passion. She dictated her mystical experiences to a cleric, who wrote them down (in Latin). The result was *The Book of Blessed Angela of Foligno*, which contains two major parts: *Memorial* and *Instructions*.

Angela's *Memorial* is her spiritual testimony and teachings on the spiritual life described as a pilgrimage—first and foremost her own journey of conversion toward a deep and intimate relationship with God, which has been described as "a spiral rather than a linear one, for in their respective journeys God and Angela come together and apart, they approach and abandon each other, so that this journey, though made of steps, is not, nor can be, a straight path."[8]

In her *Instructions*, Angela taught her followers that three forms of prayer—as revealed by divine wisdom—lead to knowledge of self and knowledge of God.[9] Physical prayer is the expression of the heart's aspirations through words and bodily motion (for example, kneeling down). Mental prayer is when our mind is in deep meditation and solely pondering the divine presence, without any distraction. And supernatural prayer is when God—who gives this gift and infuses it with divine presence—lifts the soul up so it is stretched beyond its normal limits. Then the soul understands more about God than would otherwise be possible, a "knowing" that is beyond explanation.

She further taught that these three forms of prayer would teach us who we are and who God is. And when we know who we are and who God is, we love. And when we love, we want to possess what we love. That is the sign of true love. The lover is changed—not in part but wholly—into the beloved.

Self-knowledge and self-awareness were important aspects of the inner journey for Angela of Foligno. She encouraged her followers to ponder, first of all, who and what God is. Then, experiencing a healthy, prayerful distancing from ourselves, we can see the One who is invisible, know the One who is unknowable, feel the One who is imperceptible, and thus comprehend the One who is incomprehensible. Seeing, knowing, feeling, and comprehending God, we can—each according to our unique capacity—expand in God and become filled with the divine presence through love. We find our delight in God who finds delight in us.

Beguines aspired to enter into an intense experience of the Passion and death of Christ in order to feel what he might have felt. Some of them embraced illness and harsh ascetical practices, believing that they might imitate Jesus's suffering on earth in an effort to plumb the depths of Christ's humanity at the moment of his most insistent and terrifying humanness—the moment of his dying.[10]

Beguines had a devotion to the "Wounds of Christ," a reference to the wounds Jesus suffered during his Passion and as reported in the Gospels: the nail marks in his hands and feet, the lance mark from where the centurion had thrust the lance into his side, and the head wounds from the crown of thorns that the Roman soldiers had forced onto him. Some mystics so embodied their prayerful devotion to these Wounds of Christ that they reportedly "received" the wounds themselves—they bore the stigmata. Stigmatics were revered in medieval society as particularly holy and spiritually powerful. Francis of Assisi and Marie d'Oignies were among the earliest stigmatics recorded in the history of Christianity. Among the beguines reported to be stigmatics were Ida of Louvain, Elizabeth of Spalbeek, Christine of Stommeln, and Geertrui van Oosten. But stigmatics did not necessarily bear visible wounds. Catherine of Siena's stigmata could not be seen by others, and Guglielma of Milan may have borne visible or invisible stigmata—her followers testified to both. (An invisible stigmata was understood as experiencing the pain of Crucifixion without the visible bleeding wounds.)

Most religious traditions teach and encourage healthy ascetical practices: fasting, some denial of creature comforts, committed time in prayer, and alms for the poor. Such practices can support our growth into authentic selves, cultivate compassion toward others and creation, and deepen our awareness of God's presence in our midst. Unhealthy asceticism, on the other hand, impacts our well-being, might cause self-hatred or narcissism, feeds a perverted sense of God, and weakens our relationships with others.

The majority of beguines maintained healthy ascetical practices in order to draw closer to God and to transform the world around them, and they encouraged their followers to do the same. Oftentimes beguines leading stable lives would fast on Wednesdays and Fridays, and during Advent and Lent. But some beguines were given to more frequent fasting, even when chastised by those properly concerned for their health. Out of a devotion to God they might refuse to consume anything other than the consecrated host. In medieval times, severe fasting was considered "miraculous" and a sign of God's presence. (Today we describe such practices as "holy anorexia" and understand it as a form of self-harm that denigrates the human body by destroying its health.)

Wishing to teach fellow lay seekers a path to an intimate relationship with God, beguines first and foremost taught by example. They lived, to the best of their ability, what they preached. Even their critics, being uncomfortable with beguines teaching and preaching, begrudgingly acknowledged the good that these women accomplished. Beguines were passionate in their desire to reform the church, personally and individually exhorting people to model their lives after the Gospels and the early saints. Beguines challenged, cajoled, exhorted, and prayed fervently for the continued conversion of those around them.

In one of Hadewijch's letters, she advises a young beguine to be aware that "Nowadays most people go astray, deceiving themselves that sanctity is what they long for, when in reality they are taking their ease in second-rate consolations, more is the pity. That is why you must choose and love God's will alone in all things [. . .] But today, instead of loving God's will, everyone loves himself: it is everyone's will to have peace and rest, to live with God in riches and might, and to be one with Him [Christ] in His joy and glory. We all want to be God along with God; but God knows that there are few of us who want to be man with Him [God] in His [Christ's] humanity, to carry His Cross with Him, to hang upon it with Him, to pay with Him the debt of human kind. If we look at ourselves we can see that this is true: we will not suffer anything, we will not endure. Just let our hearts be stabbed by the slightest grief, just let someone say a scornful or slanderous word about us, let anyone act against our reputation or our peace or our will, and at once we are mortally injured: we know exactly what we want and what we do not want, there are so many different things which give us pleasure or pain, now we want this and now we want that, our joy today is our sorrow tomorrow, we would like to be here, we would like to be there, we do not want something and then we want it, and in everything all we are thinking of is our own satisfaction and how we can best seek it."[11] Hadewijch's words sound very modern. She challenges her listeners to embrace the harder road to spiritual maturity.

In attempting to express the deep, heartfelt love for God, beguines felt very comfortable describing this longing for God with the sexual language found in the biblical Song of Songs. They also utilized the refined language of courtly love made popular by the troubadours. Divine Love—in the strict sense a Woman-Christ—was personified in the feminine expressions of "Caritas," "Fine Amour," or "Frau Minne." These were medieval expressions for a highly refined and exalted love, usually in reference to a love that cannot ever be consumed.

When Agnes Blannbekin referred to an intense experience of prayer she called "rapture," she taught that "the soul brings three things with her after such rapture: first, a certain noble indignation and contempt against all that is worldly and disgust against all that exists, except for God. And such contempt functions like a wall against sin. Secondly, there is a certain hidden sweetness. Thirdly, there is burning desire and languishing love for God. The first enables the soul. The second pours the soul into God, so that she will be received all the more deeply into God the more that she tastes of such lusciousness. The third illuminates the soul and makes her shine with light."[12]

Hadewijch, in her seventh vision, described a Pentecost Sunday, while her fellow beguines were singing the office of Matins: "my heart and veins and all my limbs trembled and quivered with eager desire and, as often occurred with me, such madness and fear beset my mind that it seemed to me I did not content my Beloved, and that my Beloved did not fulfill my desire, so that dying I must go mad, and going mad I must die. On that day my mind was beset so fearfully and so painfully by desirous love that all my separate limbs threatened to break and all my separate veins were in travail. The longing in which I then was cannot be expressed by any language or any person I know; and everything I could say about it would be unheard-of to all those who never apprehended Love as something to work for with desire, and whom Love had never acknowledged as hers. I can say this about it: I desired to have full fruition of my Beloved, and to understand and taste him to the full. I desired that his Humanity should to the fullest extent be one in fruition with my humanity, and that mine then should hold its stand and be strong enough to enter into perfection until I content him, who is perfect in itself, by purity and unity, and in all things to content him fully in every virtue."[13]

While many of us today might struggle to relate to such an experience of mystical love, it was very real for medieval beguines and their followers, since ardent passion toward the spiritual realm was so deeply sought by them.

Beguines presented their followers with a profound sense of the mystery of God, the *mysterium tremendum*, as well as God's deep love for humanity. The word "theology" meant "words about God based on experience." These women spoke from the depth of their experience of God, rather than from mere rational, philosophical argument. Knowledge of God was first and foremost gained in experiencing God's love and in loving God in return. Beguine mystics merged emotional and intellectual visions, thus creating new insights into the Divine. These visions were a total, embodied, and conscious experience of the Divine. God was a mystery to be pondered—with delight and respect—and beguines used startlingly sensual and homely images for the Divine such as Dance Partner, Magnet, or Ocean.

In their writings, beguines expressed an understanding of God in the language of metaphor and imagery. Marguerite Porete, for example, freely used phrases for God such as Divine Light, Power, Wisdom, and One Goodness, while Hadewijch referred to God as Wholly Other and Countenance, among other terms.

Frequently she called God Love, and she used the feminine form of the noun. Angela of Foligno spoke of God as Unknown Love.

Images are embedded with multiple meanings and open to many levels of interpretation. A language of imagery is rich and diverse and is rarely exhausted in possibilities. The power of imagery lies in its ability to speak to us in a multiplicity of meanings. Using imagery enabled the beguines to name their deeply personal experiences of God beyond bounds. God was Wholly Other, but also closest Friend and Lover; thus beguine mystics sought to find accurate and worthy expressions of their relationship with God.

Images of the Divine used by beguines included:

Music	Christ as Mother
Sweetness	Craftsman
Source of Life	Wisdom
Lover	Spouse
Fire of Love	Bridegroom
Eternal Truth	Wise Love
My Best Friend	Supreme Beauty
Gentle Lamb	Ram
Whirlpool	Fruitful Darkness
Love Alone that Suffices	The One
Ocean Depths	Fountain of Goodness
Abyss	Beloved
Dearest Love	Glowing Heart
Sweet Dew	Leader of the Dance
Resting Place	Flowing Light
The All in All	Winemaker
Abundance	All-Glorious

The dynamic sense of God that beguines expressed blended both the immanence and transcendence of the Divine.

Immanence was the very real sense of God's presence in the created world—that God can be experienced. Transcendence was the deep human awareness of the otherness of the Divine, which evokes awe and respect. Whereas many medieval theologians and preachers tended toward one of these expressions or the other, beguines mixed the two with ease. They lived with an extraordinary consciousness of the Divine, and because of the efficaciousness of their prayer, were believed to occupy that unique space between this world and the next.

Beguines had an enormous impact on laypeople's relationship to the eucharist and on what became known as eucharistic adoration. The life of Juliana of Mont-Cornillon illuminates this. Born near Liège in 1193, Juliana became an orphan at age five. She was raised by the beguine Sapientia (Latin for "wisdom"), who lived near the leper hospital at Mont-Cornillon (outside Liège). Staffed by laymen and laywomen, the hospital had been established by the burghers of Liège.

Juliana entered this mixed (and somewhat chaotic) community at Mont-Cornillon around 1207 and soon thereafter allegedly received a divine vision that would be repeated over the years: she would see the full moon shining, but the moon contained a rupture. Christ revealed to her that the moon was the church and the rupture symbolized the believers' lax attitude toward the eucharist, and he requested that a feast day be created for solemnly honoring the "Sacrament of his Body and Blood." This day was to be named Corpus Christi.

In 1222, Juliana was elected as leader of this mixed community. She tried to regularize its finances and to bring some order and discipline into the members' lifestyle. In 1237, a struggle over the finances and leadership of the community forced Juliana out, but some years later she was vindicated and she returned. In 1246,

Juliana and Canon John of Lausanne began the composition of the Office of Corpus Christi, the new liturgical feast that she believed God had called her to establish. But around 1247, due to a renewed power struggle, Juliana was forced to leave once more.

After wandering here and there for some years, Juliana and her companions—Isabella of Huy, Agnes, and Ozilia—found a safe haven at the Cistercian monastery of Salzinnes (near Namur) under its abbess Imène. They lived there as beguines until 1256, when secular politics forced both beguines and Cistercian nuns to flee. After Juliana suffered a heart attack, the exiled abbess Imène was able to locate a cell where Juliana spent her remaining days. Juliana died in 1258, reportedly on a Friday at three in the afternoon, in imitation of Christ's Passion.

Juliana was remembered for her intense devotional life focused on the human Jesus. She spoke of the "wonderful inner sweetness" she tasted when receiving the eucharist. She reportedly wept or swooned while remembering Christ's Passion and frequently enjoyed intense mystical experiences (particularly while receiving the eucharist). Her biographer reported that "when the holy Church commemorated any event at the proper time, Juliana conformed herself entirely to the season. Hence when the Church sings of Christ's Passion, she was moved with such great compassion that she could scarcely contain herself for sorrow. When she attended services she wept so profusely that the rain of tears from her eyes, squeezed from the wine-press of the Cross, copiously watered the part of the church where she was sitting. And when she heard them begin the hymn *Vexilla regis prodeunt* [The banners of the King go forth . . .], Christ's Passion was suddenly renewed for her and she cried aloud, until she had to be carried swiftly out of the church. At the remembrance of the Passion she actually melted and could not contain herself unless she was able to revive a little through such outcries, which burst forth not with the consent of her mind but from the sudden movements of her passionate heart."[14] In matching her public devotions to the liturgical season, Juliana was teaching and preaching to the public.

Juliana never ceased calling for the new feast day of Corpus Christi. Learned scholars and theologians of her day, as well as laypeople, increasingly supported her request. While Juliana did not live to see the fulfillment of her vision, Pope Urban IV did decree the celebration of the Feast of Corpus Christi in 1264.

The beguines deeply desired to experience the humanity of Jesus in the eucharist. Hadewijch described this "experiential knowing" in her seventh vision as "he [Jesus] gave himself to me in the shape of the Sacrament, in its outward form as the custom is; and then he gave me to drink from the chalice, in form and taste, as the custom is. After that he came himself to me, took me entirely in his arms, and pressed me to him; and all my members felt his full felicity, in accordance with the desire of my heart and my humanity. So I was outwardly satisfied and fully transported."[15] Beguines believed that a person "became" Christ's crucified body when receiving communion, and this for beguines was an experience of complete divine union. They taught that receiving the eucharist could be a mystical marriage and physical union with Christ.

The eucharist, for these women, was first and foremost an intense experience and not an intellectual concept. They saw and experienced Christ in the eucharist in ways that were affective, sensual, and passionate. Thus hours were spent in meditation and contemplation before the Blessed Sacrament (the consecrated host kept in a pyx or tabernacle), and this contemplative form of prayer became known as Eucharistic Adoration. The earliest evidence for this practice among beguines comes from Marie d'Oignies. It was said of Marie that the "holy bread strength-ened her heart [. . .] the holy body fattened her; the vitalizing blood purified her by washing. And she could not bear to abstain from such solace for long. For it was the same to her to live as to eat the body of Christ; and this it was to die, to be separated from the sacrament by having for a long time to abstain [. . .] And when she was not able to bear any longer her thirst for the vivifying blood, sometimes after the mass was over, she would remain for a long time contemplating the empty chalice on the altar."[16] Marie was preaching to her followers by her example.

Beguines were eager to view the host at the very moment of consecration, and many of them reported "seeing" Christ, sometimes as an infant and sometimes on the cross, at the eleva-tion of the host. While still a child, Margaret of Ypres "happened to be present when the community received the sacrament of the Lord's body, and smelled a wonderful odour. She therefore directed her attention towards it and, although she did not yet know God, yet by the interior working and manifestation of divine power she realized that Jesus, our health and salvation had come upon the altar."[17]

While in medieval times receiving the eucharist was only "required" at Christmas, Candlemas (in early February), Easter, and Pentecost, devotion to the eucharist was central to beguine spirituality at all times. Many beguines were content with gaz-ing upon the elevated host and not concerned with receiving it. Their passion was to see and gaze upon the consecrated host—not to partake. For beguines, abstaining out of awe was equal to receiving with confidence and joy. This beguine belief was a piety of presence, namely that actual reception of the eucharist was not as important as demonstrating faith in the full presence of Jesus through private prayer and worship before the conse-crated host. (Some beguines, however, did encourage frequent reception of the eucharist.) The mystical ecstasy that beguines experienced in gazing at the eucharist also served as an alternative to the authority of the priestly office.

For beguines, devotion to the body and blood of Christ was a clear affirmation of the religious significance of the human body and its emotions. Seeing the eucharist, especially at the elevation of the host, was a moment at which they were released into ecstatic union. It was a moment when the risen Christ was also supremely human and vulnerable. In an era when women enjoyed little protection under the law and little consideration by church authorities, beguines were claiming their fullest humanity through the eucharist: if God could become human, if Christ was fully present in the eucharist, then women were worthy. Thus beguines ardently believed that Christ's presence in the eucharist was an act of liberation for them, and in their contemplative devotion they could "bypass" priestly authority—especially in times of corrupt clergy and politically motivated quarrels between popes and kings.[18]

This intimate experience of contemplative gazing on the eucharist was a constant theme in beguine writings. Mechthild of Magdeburg described this experience as "pure love finds rest in God alone because these two have one will, and nobody can disturb them."[19] And it was reported of Agnes Blannbekin that "in the year of the Lord 1293 on the day of Pentecost when she [Agnes] had taken communion, she was suddenly filled with such sweetness of spirit that it spilled into her flesh in such a way that there was not one place on her whole body where she could not feel physically the invaluable sweetness. And she remained in this sweetness physically as much as spiritually for the whole day, flowing over with delights and spiritual joy."[20]

6

6\2

BEGUINE
COMPASSION

W HAT HAPPENS WHEN we die? Christianity, like many faiths, believes in life after death. The "place" of joyful eternity, where God dwells, is usually referred to as heaven or paradise; and the "place" of torment, where God is absent, is called hell. Many ancient religious traditions—for instance in Egypt and Iran, Greece and Rome—had elements in common concerning an individual's "journey from here to there." The world's faiths have sacred stories about life after death that often involve a journey or passage that transforms the individual and prepares them for eternity. This "in-between" place that offers transformation was called *Antarabhava* in Sanskrit, *Bardo* in Tibetan, *Sheol*[1] in Judaism, and purgatory in Christianity.

Many early Christians were obsessed with sin. Despite the central belief in Christ's work of salvation—that he died for our sins and rendered us worthy of being in God's presence—

church theologians over the centuries increasingly doubted that a person could enter paradise unless they managed to "make a good confession" just before death. How else could an imperfect person be allowed into the presence of God? But if God could only tolerate the presence of sinless and perfect people, as theologians claimed, how might a sinful person also be saved? By the fourth century, prominent church leaders came to believe that sinners (meaning, in their understanding, most people) could still be saved by undergoing a trial after death— a purgative phase—to extinguish lingering sin and prepare them to dwell in God's presence.

Purgatory was traditionally understood as "the condition of suffering, both punitive and redemptive, undergone by elect souls between the moment of death and their eventual admission to heaven."[2] Some modern scholars suggest that by the end of the twelfth century, the concept of purgatory[3] had grown to be a "third place" of spatial embodiment alongside earth and heaven/hell. While theologians of the first millennium had suggested that purgatory might be a quickened process, lasting perhaps only a flash of time after death, by the 1100s purgatory was understood to be a place of fire where sins were purged so that the deceased could eventually enter heaven. Even though sins could be forgiven during a person's lifetime by making confession, with penance assigned by the priest hearing the confession, what happened if there was insufficient time to fulfill this penance before death? Purgatory was believed to be the place where penance for sin could be fulfilled. And rather than purgation happening in a flash, the "time" spent in purgatory took on an earthly sense: days and months and years of suffering. However, the medieval church also taught that people could pray for souls in purgatory and that their prayers would effectively aid those souls in their transition from purgatory to heaven.

Beguines, as we have seen, were understood to have extraordinary spiritual powers. People believed that having a beguine intercede before God on their behalf was an assurance that their petition was heard by God—and perhaps in no instance more than for "those poor souls in purgatory." And beguines believed that they did indeed exercise the authority to release countless souls from purgatory. Many of the stories included in the vitae of beguines grapple with the fate of the deceased in purgatory (or hell).

In the *Life of Marie d'Oignies*, for example, we are told that one day when Marie "was in her cell adjacent to the church at Oignies, she saw a multitude of hands before her as if in supplication. Amazed and not knowing what this vision was, she was struck by some little fear and fled to the church. On another occasion when she was in her cell, she once again saw these same hands and was terrified, but when she again fled to the church, she was held back and detained by the hands. Then she ran to the church as though the church itself were a tabernacle so that she might have counsel from the Lord. She begged the Lord that he tell her what it was those hands wanted of her. The Lord replied that the tortured souls of the dead in purgatory were asking for the prayers of her intercession that would soothe their sufferings as if these prayers were a precious ointment. Then, because of the sweetness of this contemplation, she interrupted her usual prayers for a time and could neither open her mouth nor think of anything except God."[4]

Lutgard of Aywières (1182–1246) was known as the patron saint of purgatory. Her contemporaries considered her a profound yet unpretentious woman with a ministry as a spiritual director, prophet, much sought-after healer and intercessor (especially on behalf of sinners and souls suffering in purgatory), and exorcist.

Born in Tongeren, she began as a beguine of St. Catherine in the nearby town of Sint-Truiden in 1194. Then, sometime between 1200 and 1205, she helped establish a Benedictine monastery for which she reluctantly accepted the duties as prioress. Tiring of the responsibilities of leadership and hoping for more time for prayer, Lutgard transferred in 1210 to a newly established Cistercian monastery at Aywières (today the village of Awirs, near Liège) where, allegedly, she hoped her French would be so insufficient that she would never be elected to office. Evidently Lutgard was seeking to avoid responsibilities as prioress. All along, she remained in close contact with beguines.

In 1216, Lutgard began the first of three seven-year fasts while also having to move three times, always in search of a permanent home. She dedicated her first fast to the conversion of Albigensian heretics. Her second fast was intended for the conversion of sinners in general. And the third fast was on behalf of the church, which she thought might be compromised by a looming political alliance (probably between Emperor Frederick II and the Tartars). These three seven-year fasts also gave Lutgard's biographer, Thomas of Cantimpré (c. 1200–c. 1265/70), a framework to shape her *Vita* into three parallel periods: as a spiritual beginner —beguine and Benedictine—which was also her period of most intense visionary experience; as an advanced contemplative and Cistercian; and lastly as a perfected saint.[5] The much younger Thomas saw himself as her "spiritual son" and protégé and eventually composed Lutgard's *Vita*.

An apostle, in the Christian tradition, was one sent to share the Christian message. Lutgard's message was meant for sinners without hope of salvation and for souls suffering in purgatory— Marie d'Oignies saw Lutgard as the most powerful and efficacious intercessor in delivering souls from purgatory. Lutgard's *Vita* richly describes her ability to see the state of a person's salvation and then, like a physician, offer the most appropriate cure: calling the person to repentance, countering their despair with the hope of God's consolation, or recommending prayer and fasting so that God might forgive the person. Her *Vita* reported that Lutgard was visited—straight from purgatory—by Abbot Simon of Foigny, Pope Innocent III, Duchess Mary of Brabant, Jacques de Vitry, and by her own sister, all of them seeking Lutgard's assistance for their release into heaven.

Thomas described, in Book II of Lutgard's *Vita*,[6] that she would hear "the cry of Christ's wounds" as they perpetually bled on behalf of sinners—the allusion being that, because of human sin, Jesus was still being crucified. In one reported vision, Lutgard was taken up to heaven where she beheld Christ prostrate before the Father, making impassioned entreaties for the souls of God's children. Christ then turned to Lutgard and commissioned her to return to earth and do likewise. Lutgard was believed to serve as a "co-redeemer," meaning that alongside Jesus she could suffer redemptively on behalf of others (through her prayers and tears and fasts) and thus allow sinners to get into heaven. Thomas reported that Lutgard would negotiate with heaven on behalf of sinners, fasting and praying until she received a direct answer from God.

Witnesses to Lutgard's embodied visions claimed that whenever her visions involved a reenacting of the Passion, her whole body would turn red as if drenched in blood. One witness, a trustworthy priest, had crept up silently in the chapel where Lutgard was leaning against a wall, deep in contemplative prayer. This priest, to test the veracity of what he saw, clipped a snippet of her blood-soaked hair. When Lutgard came out of her rapture and the blood "disappeared" off her body and clothing, the priest saw that her lock of hair, too, had returned to its natural color.[7]

Lutgard embraced a devotion to the sacred heart of Jesus, a metaphor for compassion. This choice was directly connected to her ministry to souls in purgatory: both were grounded in deep and abiding compassion. After her death (as her spirit allegedly told a friend soon afterward) she felt such compassion as she passed by the souls in purgatory that God allowed a whole company of them to follow her into paradise.[8]

In the medieval world, the realm of purgatory was very familiar. People were intensely aware, and felt a real presence, of those who had died, and they frequented cemeteries to "visit family." They also often attended mass and said many prayers on behalf of those whom they loved and feared were suffering the flames of purgatory. Medieval people were equally aware of the very real presence of an evil force that sought to undermine the foundations of civil society, sow the seeds of disbelief and blasphemy, and lead the faithful away from salvation and into damnation. Ghosts and evil spirits were seen as real, and men and women alike felt utterly powerless against these realities. To whom could they turn for help?

Beguines exercised the greatest power and pastoral compassion in dealing with purgatory, more than clerics and monastics. Church leaders and laity alike knew without doubt that beguines held the power to release souls from purgatory due to the efficacy of their prayer. Beguines exercised deep compassion when they accepted requests to intercede before God on behalf of people believed to be suffering and languishing in purgatory, and as reported in some vitae and visions, beguines "negotiated" successfully with God over the fate of souls in purgatory.

While rules of life among beguine communities varied, one common thread was the commitment to pray for souls in purgatory and to offer acts of asceticism (such as self-denial, fasting, and almsgiving) to seek the release of souls from purgatory. For example, the thirteenth-century *Règle des Fins Amans*, a rule of life composed for some French beguines, mentions a duty to pray for the dead who await mercy so that God may relieve their torment and hasten their glory.[9] A series of sermons on purgatory was given in 1272/73 to the beguines at St. Catherine in Paris by Gilles d'Orléans. These sermons closely reflected how beguines themselves perceived purgatory. Three aspects of it were emphasized: purgatory was God's prison, and thus the beguines had a duty to pray for souls in prison (this practice harks back to the ancient tradition of praying for Christians in Roman prisons during times of persecution); purgatory established solidarity between the living and the dead; and purgatory was closely related to penance—either penance delivered the soul from purgatory, or purgatory completed the penitential process.[10] (Sermons of this magnitude might have been a collaboration between preachers and beguines, since through these sermons a preacher was publicly establishing and affirming the beguine ministry of aiding souls in purgatory.)

Clearly, the beguine understanding of purgatory was primarily pastoral. They were passionately interested in reforming the lives of their followers and neighbors, calling each to a life of prayer, integrity, and compassion. As mentioned, certain beguines exercised the gift of "reading souls"—being able to identify a person's state of salvation and confronting unconfessed sins. At times a beguine, after receiving a vision, "pursued" notorious sinners, calling them to turn their lives around. The beguine's intent was to encourage the person to reform their life and draw closer to God. Yet beguines understood human nature—people would falter and fall back into sin—and thus they encouraged their followers to trust in God's love for them. It was a natural extension of their overall ministry to offer compassion to souls suffering in purgatory.

Marie d'Oignies pursued her friends to help her pray for souls separated from God in purgatory. Mechthild of Magdeburg prayed for a vast number of people she "saw" dwelling in purgatory, including a friar, a beguine, a priest, and a thoroughly immoral victim of murder. Mechthild prayed, "Give me, O Holy One, the guilty souls out of purgatory; on me alone be their ransom."[11] Rixenda, a beguine of Narbonne in southern France, testified that around 1280 she had been "carried off to heaven and there saw Jesus both standing and seated and his mother Mary right next to him and nearby Saint Francis [. . .] She saw her father and mother in Purgatory in the process of expiating their sins . . . and they said that thanks to her prayers many souls are taken from Purgatory, especially her father and mother and a cousin, Aucradis. She also said that in her flight she saw a woman, Feralguière of Béziers, overburdened with punishments in Purgatory, thrashed and beaten for three days . . . She saw her father and mother at the Gate of Heaven, and shortly thereafter they were received into their mansion."[12]

Beguines so passionately "interacted" with purgatory that it was reported that some of them could cross from this world into the next, intercede before God on behalf of a tormented soul, and win their release into paradise. As we saw with Lutgard, some beguines were seen as a kind of "co-redeemer" with Jesus. Just as beguines "shared" in Christ's Passion and Crucifixion through their embodied prayer experiences, they also "shared" in Christ's redemptive sequel—the belief that, after Jesus's death, he had visited hell and released all souls who wanted to join him in paradise. Numerous visions of beguines reported that they descended into hell in order to retrieve a soul or, at least, to alleviate the suffering of those who had died in a state of sin but wanted to enter heaven. Some beguines reported seeing a deceased person in purgatory who begged them to pray for the person's release from purgatory, while others reported receiving revelations of divine justice that awaited a person living in sin. These beguines then felt compelled to warn the sinners of the punishment that awaited them if they did not change their ways. Tellingly, while beguines were chastised for teaching and preaching and leading independent lives, their ministry as "co-redeemer" with Jesus in regard to souls in purgatory was never questioned by church authorities. Churchmen, too, needed any help they could get to enter heaven.

The belief in purgatory embodied an overwhelming place in the visions, devotions, and ministry of beguines, which one scholar describes as "purgatorial piety."[13] Ultimately, they understood purgatory to be about love. Medieval religious piety believed that burning in purgatory caused purification (while burning in hell caused eternal torment). In paradise, this burning flame was actually eternal light and love. Thus the seeker was encouraged not to abandon hope but to embrace the call to conversion and transformation while still alive, to review one's faults, cultivate faith, and pursue love.

The pain and suffering that beguines felt—not being able to experience God as deeply and fully as they wanted—was viscerally real for them. They felt as if they were in purgatory *now*, experiencing the burning separation from God, their Beloved. Their hopeful attitude toward purgatory was grounded in their belief that the process of purgatory would lead them closer to God. Catherine of Genoa spoke of experiencing "the fiery love of God, a love that consumed her [Catherine], cleansing and purifying all, so that once quitted this life she could appear forthwith in God's presence."[14] This hope for purification in order to experience God more fully was profoundly real to beguines. Marguerite Porete proclaimed that "Truth tells my heart I am loved by Someone who cares for me unconditionally. This gift delights me past the point of thinking. It transforms me, too, and I become one with divine Love, who reminds me. She enters me and loves in me, and gives me the strength to do whatever She wants. The divine Lover gives me this spiritual power."[15]

Beguines believed that purgatory deepened one's capacity to experience and dwell with God; they taught that purgatory was about love—God "allowed" purgatory to exist so that ultimately humans could spend eternity with God. While the church was emphasizing "Divine Justice" and "Divine Retribution," literally preaching "brimstone and fire," beguines were torn. On one hand, God was right to demand justice because humanity, in its sinning, had disobeyed God. On the other hand, the God who is Love could not possibly want anyone to remain in hell. At times beguines felt scandalous in "defying" God's "right" to demand justice from a sinner because they would accept onto themselves—on behalf of the sinner—the "punishment owed." Yet beguines explained that Love impelled them to assume this burden, believing that God's love, rather than hell, would ultimately prevail.

God is Love. Beguines understood the depth of this reality to the point that they could, with Hadewijch, say that no one need to fear hell because even the path into hell ultimately leads to God. Beguine writings reveal some women "negotiating hell away from God" because they could not imagine God who is Love tolerating souls suffering in hell. Distancing themselves from the growing comfort of medieval men and women with indulgences (buying or earning one's way into heaven), beguines taught that people should not serve others out of hope of earning entry into heaven that way—because God's love could not be bought with money or earned with good deeds.

Beguines dedicated themselves frequently to penance, such as long fasts and hours spent in intercessory prayer, on behalf of those doomed and in need of God's mercy. These women also, through their embodied experiences of prayer that often included visionary experiences, claimed that they entered purgatory and willingly suffered alongside the person on whose behalf they were interceding. Family members might seek out a beguine known for her ecstatic visions to inquire about a deceased relative and to ask for her help in winning the relative's release from purgatory. This visionary, together with her fellow beguines, would then begin to "pour out" prayers to God and undertake to suffer the torments of the deceased, as a form of embodied intercessory prayer, to alleviate the dead person's suffering. This prayer was understood as an active and divine process.

Agnes Blannbekin saw purgatory as a place that was neither the torment of hell nor the beatific vision of the resurrected Christ, but rather a state of in-between existence. She recounted a vision where "she [Agnes] was led underneath the earth to nice enough places, where a large group of shimmering human beings with adorned faces appeared who, like mutes, did not speak. As she was taught later on, these were the dead who had died without grave sins. They did not receive any other punishment than the lack of the vision of God. But as she herself said, this punishment was the worst to them."[16]

The beguine Christina the Astonishing had a near-death experience in 1182. Her biographer wrote that Christina—after dying and visiting hell, purgatory, and heaven—came back to life with great zeal to free souls from purgatory. This mission became the central focus of her ministry. She taught that "nothing made God weep more with mercy for sinners than when sinners are moved by mercy toward their neighbors, for mercy and pity never can result in anything but good at the last day."[17] Christina, who was a friend of Lutgard, willingly sought out opportunities for suffering on behalf of souls in purgatory or hell and for those whose life on earth was leading them toward damnation; she would act out this suffering to make its tortures visible on earth, hopefully winning the conversion of sinners. She reportedly received daily revelations from God concerning the spiritual peril of persons who were about to die, whom she would then visit and exhort to turn their lives toward God and away from sin. Christina's power over purgatory was considered so efficacious that Count Louis of Loon made his deathbed confession to her and not to a priest.

Catherine of Genoa (1447–1510) was an Italian penitent woman whose compassionate and insightful treatise, *Purgation and Purgatory*, revealed her refreshing vision of the pure love of God for the soul. She believed that our soul freely enters this process of purgation in order to achieve the purity necessary for union with God. She exhorted seekers to embrace this process of purgation and, in embracing God's mercy, not to live with guilt for past error and sin. Catherine described a relationship of perfect trust and conformity to the divine will[18] and alluded to the hope of pure union with God.

Catherine was born into the aristocratic Fieschi family in Genoa and married into another aristocratic family, the Adorno, in 1463. She lived in the midst of power and privilege in an unhappy marriage; her husband, Giuliano, was dissolute and unfaithful.

Catherine suffered from intense loneliness and depression, but in 1473 she experienced a radical conversion with an overwhelming sense of God's love and mercy. Her depression gave way to an intensely interior time of contemplative prayer, yet she also felt a strong need to actively service the sick and poor. Surprisingly, Giuliano, too, came to experience an authentic conversion, became a Franciscan tertiary, and spent the remainder of his life working alongside Catherine caring for the destitute. Together they worked at Genoa's Pammatone Hospital, where Catherine served as director from 1490 to 1496.

The plague struck Genoa in 1493, killing a great number of its inhabitants, including Giuliano. Catherine converted the outdoor area behind the Pammatone into additional hospital space and supervised the care of the patients.

Purgation and Purgatory is Catherine's account of her own spiritual purification that she described as a fiery love, a love that consumed her in a cleansing and purifying sense so that she might one day be ready to experience the fullness of God's presence in the life to come. Her other work, *The Spiritual Dialogue*, is more of a spiritual autobiography, a story of her inner life. In its writing she was influenced by the Scriptures, the poetry of the Franciscan Jacopone da Todi, and devotional writings on Dionysius by her friend Tommasa Fiesca, an Augustinian nun.

Essentially, Catherine taught that God is Pure Love and the object of our total fulfillment, but that the spiritual life as a process or journey—growing from self-will into pure love—is not easy and continues after our death. One of her most famous teachings is: "God is my being, my me, my strength, my happiness, my good, my delight . . . I will have nothing to do with a love that would be *for* God or *in* God. I cannot bear the word *for* or the word *in*, because they denote something that may be in between God and me. This is the love that pure love cannot bear since pure love is Godself."[19]

Motivated by their deep and compassionate love for their fellow believers, beguines gave hope to many. They offered their own prayers and penances on behalf of others, pulling (according to the common belief) poor souls out of the flames of purgatory and thrusting them into the presence of God. Thanks to the beguines, people did not need to feel utterly helpless when wondering about the state of their beloved who had died or contemplating their very own salvation. Beguines could and would intercede on their behalf.

7

BEGUINES AS PREACHERS AND PERFORMERS

W HILE LUTGARD OF AYWIÈRES was known as the patron saint of purgatory, it was her friend Christina (c. 1150– 1224), called the Astonishing or Christina Mirabilis, whose life was one of continuous preaching of purgatory. Considered a beguine by her contemporaries (and also by modern scholars), her story nevertheless stretches our understanding of what constituted a beguine. Like many beguines, she preached and pursued the salvation of souls with great passion. Yet the extreme nature of Christina's preaching and sacred performance (meaning she also acted out her preaching, much of which is rather challenging for modern ears) reveals a woman unconcerned with her reputation. Utterly motivated by her love for God and fellow women and men, she was willing to be perceived as a fool if it meant people might reform their lives.

The youngest of three sisters, Christina was born in the village of Brustem near Sint-Truiden to a family of modest means and spent her childhood tending the family's flock. After the death of her parents, she and her sisters decided to live as lay religious.

In 1182 Christina, according to her *Vita*, "died" after having been gravely ill. During her funeral mass she reportedly stirred in her coffin and then rose, floating to the rafters of the church. There she remained, immovable, until the Agnus Dei was chanted and her body returned to the ground. Christina later explained that during her "death" she had seen a terrifying place where the souls of the dead, including people she knew, were cruelly tormented. An angel told her this place was purgatory. Afterward Christina was taken to paradise. She was given the choice of staying in heaven or returning to earth to assist those in purgatory. With her return to earth, and coming back from the dead during her funeral service, her life as a roaming preacher had begun.

Thomas of Cantimpré reported in his *Vita* of Christina that, after she had "died" and ascended to heaven, Christ had requested that she return to earth and "endure purgatory" while living in the world. From around 1210 to 1218 she lived intermittently with the recluse Jutta at Borgloon (near Sint-Truiden). Christina was supported by family and friends and she also begged, which for her was a deliberate form of humiliation.

Christina's entire presence was a sermon on purgatory. She did not merely preach, but acted out what she was trying to convey as she attempted to save souls and convert her audience. This mission to "live purgatory on earth" was Thomas of Cantimpré's[1] explanation for Christina's most unusual behavior. She allegedly threw herself into hot ovens, placed her hands and feet into fires, jumped into boiling cauldrons, stood in frigid waters in the dead of winter, hung herself on gibbets, and even entered tombs—possibly in order to preach to the dead as well.

Christina was reportedly quite jarring and demonstrative in her embodied preaching. She captured and sustained the attention of her audience, who clearly grasped the moral of her parable. Once, upon entering a church, it was reported that she "threw herself before the altar as if she were a sack filled with dry bones. Then, wailing bitterly, she began to beat her breast and her body most often and said, 'O miserable and wretched body! How long will you torment me, miserable as I am? What are you doing with me? Why do you keep my wretched soul in you for so long? Why do you delay me from seeing the face of Christ? When will you abandon me so that my soul can return freely to its Creator? Woe to you, most miserable one! And woe to me who am united to you!'"[2] She was enacting purgatory for her audience with the intent of shaking them awake to the consequences of their sinful life and illustrating what the experience of purgatory might be for them. Given her popularity, she clearly got their attention.

As the years went by, Christina's extraordinary acts of penance subsided and a period of rapt visions ensued—and these visions did not occur in solitude but always in public. It was said that in her embodied visions, Christina was leading the souls of the dead as far as purgatory, or through purgatory as far as the realm of heaven, without any harm to herself. With both her public acts of penance and her visions she was preaching a powerful message.

Christina frequently preached through singing. Once, while visiting the Benedictine nuns at St. Catherine's near Sint-Truiden and speaking of Christ, the nuns reported that "suddenly and unexpectedly she [Christina] would be ravished in the spirit and her body would whirl around like a hoop in a children's game. She whirled around with such extreme violence that the individual limbs of her body could not be distinguished. When she had whirled around for a long time in this manner, it seemed as if she became weakened by the violence of the rolling and all her limbs grew quiet. Then there sounded between her throat and her breast a wondrous harmony that no mortal man could understand, nor could it be imitated by any artificial instrument. That song of hers had only the pliancy and the tones of music. But the words of the melody, so to speak—if they could even be called words—sounded together incomprehensibly. No sound or breath came out of her mouth or nose during this time, but a harmony of the angelic voice resounded only from between her breast and throat."[3] Christina then concluded her "miraculous" sermon (what we would essentially call singing in tongues or glossolalia today) with singing the Te Deum laudamus.

Christina made purgatory immanent and real to her audience. She proclaimed through her embodied reenactments what the church would never allow her to preach from a pulpit, and she left her audience in awe. In their understanding, the miracles God performed through Christina's life were a sacramental witness for all, testifying to God's deep love for humanity.

Christina the Astonishing died at the monastery of St. Catherine's during a visit. Yet she was not done preaching. Seven years after her death, her tomb was opened and many who were present for this testified to spiritual and physical healing. While many legends of saints have the holy one fleeing society to seek God, Christina was understood to have fled from God into the world in order to ensure that others would be able to enjoy God's presence as well. Christina was indeed astonishing.

Beguines and their medieval audiences were familiar with dramatic performances, both to entertain and to educate. Frequently a symbiosis existed between secular and religious drama. Miracle plays, morality plays, plays enacting stories from the Bible (especially in Christmas pageants and Passion plays), as well as mystery plays were common. Beguines were adept at using this interactive medium to present their teachings and to exhort their audiences to a deeper spiritual life. Mechthild of Magdeburg and Marguerite Porete wrote in the form of dialogue, with the probable intent of sacred performance. Beatrijs of Nazareth and Hadewijch described their visions in such a way that they could be enacted as sacred theater. Other beguines took familiar gospel stories and performed them for small groups, at chapel gatherings, and on public squares. A particularly popular choice was the reenactment of Christ's Passion and Crucifixion.

Beguines walked the streets, calling people to reform their ways, sometimes carrying a crude wooden cross. They created elaborate puppet shows, read their poetry aloud, and were gifted storytellers. People would have experienced a preaching beguine as a flesh-and-blood sermon, as a performed commentary or homily on the gospel story. Beguines were preaching in every creative form they could conceive.

The church politics of imposing interdict in order to gain obedience from a monarch—the pope would command a "spiritual" punishment for a diocese or realm—denied the laypeople living there contact with their clergy. Churches might be closed for months or even years, denying to anybody who was not a cleric or monastic access to the proclaiming of Scripture, preaching, and the sacraments. This denial of everyday religious life was a brutal reality beguines could not tolerate. So they chose to fill the spiritual void caused by an interdict with their own proclamations and preaching, in their own chapels and in the local square. Beguines were eager to aid in the spiritual transformation of their followers, and by preaching through performance—acting and dancing and singing—they were performing their theology as well as embodying their mysticism.

The performers of a religious play and their captivated audience entered fully into the experience of a sacred story come to life, and all of them were transformed. Sacred performances were efficacious, meaning that both actor and audience were deeply touched and each departed a somewhat different person through a broadened perspective or deepened compassion.

In their sacred performances, beguine mystics were "making present," "making real" the original mystical experience of God. The intent was to teach and preach the gospel and to remind their audience of God's profound love and mercy for them. While the presentation of the sacred material had been rehearsed by the beguines and was not necessarily spontaneous, no amount of planning and rehearsal could reduce the powerful creativity of their live performances.

Elizabeth of Spalbeek (c. 1246–1304), whose preaching and performing apostolate took place almost entirely in her small local chapel (attached to which she lived in a cell, with a large window onto the altar), was extraordinarily popular. She is believed to have attracted audiences from far and wide who came to witness her vivid reenactments—in the form of pantomime—of Christ's Passion. And this despite her apparent lack of physical strength, which meant she could hardly leave her cell without assistance. In addition to her performances, Elizabeth was known, as were so many beguines, for her ability to read souls and give spiritual counsel.

Born into a noble family, Elizabeth lived in this cell in the village of Spalbeek outside Hasselt (Belgium). Her mother and sisters lived nearby and a cousin, William of Ryckel, the Benedictine abbot of Sint-Truiden, served as her protector. Abbot William, a supporter of the beguines (he established the beguinage St. Agnes at Sint-Truiden in 1258), enjoyed powerful political connections as secretary and chaplain to William II of Holland.

The Cistercian abbot Philip of Clairvaux visited Spalbeek around 1267 and wrote an account of his observation of Elizabeth's sacred pantomime. She preached the Passion of Christ through her silent reenactment, playing each character—Jesus, his various tormentors, Mary, onlookers—with marvelous attention to detail, inviting her audience to palpably enter into the experience of the Passion.

As was common in medieval times, Abbot Philip described Elizabeth's performance within the timeframe of the book of hours (or Divine Office): Matins (midnight) was associated with the Agony in the Garden; Lauds (sunrise) with the Betrayal; Prime (6 a.m.) with Christ's appearance before Pilate; Terce (9 a.m.) with the Flagellation; Sext (at noon) with the Carrying of the Cross; None (3 p.m.) with the Crucifixion; Vespers (sunset) with the Deposition (removal of the body from the cross); and Compline (evening) with the Entombment.[4]

Abbot Philip described Elizabeth as rising "at midnight to acknowledge the beginning of the Lord's Passion—that is, how He was arrested, how He was forcibly pulled away, and how He was dragged most cruelly by the hands of the impious. I should not neglect to say that in this hour, as in the other hours, she is entranced (in rapture or ecstasy) before she rises, and she remains wholly rigid in the same position in which she is entranced (in rapture or ecstasy) for a long time, like an image of wood or of stone without sense or motion or breath, so that no part of her can be touched or moved, not even her little finger, unless her whole body is moved. After this trance, as though returned to herself, she rises and quickly leaves her bed and strides through her room in a wondrous and orderly way."[5]

After coming out of such a prayerful trance, Elizabeth would begin to walk around her cell and silently express anguish and pain. Abbot Philip explained that "previously feeling nothing, she celebrated the *memory* of the Lord's Passion through her *actions*; now, however, she expresses the *actual* pain of His suffering through her own immediate pain by actually *suffering with Him* [. . .] she is not able to walk, nor is she able even to rise to her feet, but instead she turns and rolls over the ground. She also frequently bangs her head on the ground with hard blows, and she almost continuously twists her head, hands, and arms, lamentably distorting her whole body in a manner I cannot describe. She frequently utters groans and nearly mortal sobs among her pains as if she were experiencing not merely the pains of a woman in labor but rather the pains of one dying."[6]

Elizabeth was the exemplar stigmatic, allegedly exhibiting bleeding wounds like Christ's on her hands, feet, and side.[7] It was said that on Fridays she would receive the stigmata; at None, blood mixed with water flowed from her side. On Good Friday in 1266 she allegedly suffered the crushing pain and bleeding as if enduring the crown of thorns, thereby transforming herself as a means of preaching into a living Christ crucified. Abbot Philip (who had no problem understanding Elizabeth's silent message) wrote that "in her stigmata and pains she teaches faith in the Passion; in her joy and cheerfulness after pain, she teaches faith in the Resurrection; in her trances, faith in the ascension; in her shame and revelations and spiritual life, faith in the mission of the Holy Ghost. The things said above demonstrate enough about her feelings for the sacraments of the altar and of confession and about her desire for the salvation of all and about her sorrow over humanity's ingratitude and loss of absolution. How inexcusable are you, O man, if such extraordinary living and manifest arguments do not excite you to strength of faith and to love of charity and to practice of devotion!"[8]

The aim of much of Elizabeth's preaching was the reform of neglectful and indifferent clergy. Her movements and expressions were intended to challenge her audience, many of whom were priests, to truly value and understand what Jesus had experienced. The clergy's preaching ought to convey an immediacy, a gratitude for the Passion story. She even challenged Abbot Philip with these rare spoken words: "you ought to be very attentive in the praise of God, and in preaching His name, and in directing souls to salvation."[9]

Rose of Viterbo (c. 1233–1251) was a penitentia in central Italy whose short life belies the duration of her reputation for holiness. She reportedly walked through the streets of Viterbo carrying a cross and exhorting the crowds to greater virtue. The *Vita* of Rose, written to establish a case for her sanctity, said that she preached the Word of God to large crowds of men and women but without church approval. Viterbo was caught in the middle of a great power struggle between Emperor Frederick II and the pope. Mendicant preachers and clerics were equally passionate in fighting for what was in their own best interests, and charges of heresy flew. Rose preached on behalf of the gospel and avoided a political position. At one point she and her family were driven from Viterbo because she did not take sides, but she continued her preaching in the countryside. Significantly, Rose was never questioned or condemned for her preaching by church authorities, perhaps because the power of her sanctity had overcome any doubt about her legitimacy as preacher.

Douceline of Digne was likewise a powerful public preacher. She frequently used her visions as a springboard for her preaching and was known to interact with her audience with questions and answers. At times she spontaneously chanted some of her insights in liturgical form and incorporated sophisticated and complex dance movements during her preaching. Douceline's preaching on the Trinity (the Holy Spirit in particular) and on poverty was collected and preserved by her followers.

Beguines preached often on the Holy Trinity. For example, Mechthild of Magdeburg spoke of "God as One and Undivided in Three Persons, and the Three Persons as one Undivided God."[10] When beguines spoke publicly of the Holy Trinity, it usually earned them especially harsh criticism, since medieval theologians considered Trinitarian theology—among all areas of theology—the one area women were least capable of teaching. Marguerite Porete, in her work *The Mirror of Simple Souls*, spoke of the Trinity as "Power, Wisdom and Goodness," as "One Power, One Wisdom, One Will," and as "Lover, Loved and Love," then expanded this explanation to "eternal substance, pleasing fruition, and loving conjunction."[11] In describing her experience of mature contemplation, Hadewijch (in her twenty-eighth letter) spoke of experiencing God's Eternity and Greatness and Wisdom and Nobility as well as Presence, Effusion, and Totality.

Agnes Blannbekin, like Douceline, exemplified preaching in public by living the devotion she wanted her followers to embrace, such as frequent visits to churches and daily attendance at mass. Her visions reportedly occurred during mass or in quiet prayer after mass, and also during her private prayer at home, and her visions then nurtured her preaching.

In one vision, according to Agnes, on the third day of Pentecost she saw the Risen Christ, naked and standing with arms raised to midbody and hands extended like a priest at the altar, and surrounded by the saints. She described a golden flame emanating from all around Christ, like rays pointing toward heaven and down to the center of the earth and also piercing human beings. She said that she did not understand this vision until one of the rays of the flame penetrated her chest, set her heart on fire in divine love, and illuminated her heart. She then described the different ways these rays touched people: sometimes one ray penetrated many people, sometimes one person was touched by many rays, and some people were not touched by rays at all.

Agnes stated that this golden flame was the grace of the Holy Spirit that flows out from Christ: the flame piercing the earth signifies grace that visits all the elect in purgatory; the flame spread out above the earth among human beings symbolizes the grace distributed among good human beings still living on earth; the flame entering through the crown of the head symbolizes the grace that elevates the mind to that which is above and that sweetens the soul with the sweetness of divine comfort; the flame that moves through the ears signifies the grace of the Holy Spirit poured into a person and comforting the soul through the words of a sermon. Yet the flame infused through the mouth symbolizes the grace poured into a person through prayer, which makes a prayer savory and brings forth devotion, and the flame permeating the chest signifies the grace of the Holy Spirit that inflames the human heart to the love of God and illuminates the intellect.[12]

Agnes, like other beguines, was considered a "liturgical visionary," meaning that her visions and her subsequent preaching were connected to the church's liturgical calendar (with which her audience would have been intimately familiar). Hadewijch, too, was a liturgical visionary, and in her seventh vision we hear that "on a certain Pentecost Sunday I had a vision at dawn. Matins were being sung in the church, and I was present. My heart and my veins and all my limbs trembled and quivered from desire; and as had been usual with me such madness and fear befell me that I thought I could not satisfy my love and that my Beloved did not fulfill my love, so that I, dying, would go mad, and going mad, I would die."[13] What did her fellow worshipers think of Hadewijch as she was trembling and quivering and feeling like she was going insane? Her audience must have understood that she was preaching through her vision. The power of the vision given by God became the authority by which these beguines preached.

One of the greatest woman mystics and preachers in the Middle Ages was Catherine of Siena.[14] She was born into a large Sienese family in 1347, and already as a girl sought a life dedicated to prayer and asceticism. At fifteen she cut off her hair, an act of defiance that declared she would not marry. She began a life of solitude, silence, and harsh asceticism in her family home, including physical mortification and severe fasting, all of which resulted in compromising her health. She then became a Dominican tertiary (called a Mantellata in Siena).

Although now counting herself among the local Mantellate, Catherine continued her life of intense prayer and ascetical practices. But after she experienced a dramatic vision around the age of twenty, she realized that the place of a contemplative was not to escape into solitude but to live out and about with those in deepest need. She now began her very public life and ministry. While serving the poor and destitute she also availed herself of opportunities to hear theologians and preachers. Soon her insatiable hunger for knowledge and understanding drew the attention of many people, and her avid followers included other young women with a desire to serve God, along with Dominican friars and others.

In 1374, Raymond of Capua (c. 1330–1399) was appointed by the master of the Dominican Order to serve as Catherine's confessor and mentor. In Raymond she found an ideal partner—intellectually, spiritually, and politically—and he encouraged her to take her public ministry beyond the region of Siena. Thus her renowned gift for conciliation was put to work mediating political peace among the city-states of Italy and attempting to bring the papacy from its exile in Avignon back to Rome.

Although she was the daughter of a dyer and never attended formal school, Catherine had learned to read during her years of intense solitude. She absorbed biblical and liturgical texts in Latin, along with the vernacular works of the popular religious writers of her day. She had the intellectual ability to absorb and integrate insights from a broad range of sources and to reshape them into her own patterns, interrelationships, and images.

Around 385 *Letters* dictated by Catherine survive to this day. Recipients included popes, cardinals and bishops, royalty and public officials, family and friends and disciples, allies and opponents, political prisoners, and others. These *Letters* advocated for peace, pressed for personal improvement as well as reform of the church, and urged support for her causes. Catherine's *Letters* were clearly a form of public preaching, as she knew they were being read aloud, copied, and disseminated among her followers.

Her *Letters* also offered spiritual counsel and consolation, both to dear friends and followers as well as to people who sought her counsel but did not know her personally. She taught that self-knowledge was the path to God and encouraged each person to learn about God's immense love for them. In one letter she stated that "in self-knowledge you will find the gentle mercy of the Holy Spirit, the aspect of God that gives and is nothing but love. Whatever the Spirit does is done for love. You'll find the Spirit's movement of love within your own soul because our will is nothing but love, and its every affection and movement comes from nothing but love."[15]

Over several months in 1377 and 1378, Catherine dictated the summation of her understanding of a soul's journey to God into a single narrative known as *The Dialogue*. While she used refreshingly original imagery, her style was that of a preacher, not a poet. Catherine's *Dialogue*, like her *Letters*, reveals a genius for applying theological and dogmatic abstractions to the everyday concerns of regular people. While her contemporaries agreed that Catherine experienced many mystical and ecstatic visions, her mysticism was grounded explicitly in her conviction that the quest for God was inseparable from an active compassion for the world.[16]

As was the case for many beguines, Catherine's sense of God was extraordinarily positive. "You're the highest, infinite God. You're good above every good. You're joyous good. You're good beyond measure and understanding. You're beauty above every other sort of beauty. You're wisdom above all wisdom. You're wisdom itself and the food of angels, and You are given to us with a burning love. You're the clothes that cover all nakedness. You pasture the starving within Your sweetness. How sweet You are, God, with no hint of bitterness!"[17]

Catherine of Siena died in Rome in 1380, exhausted by her passionate work and ascetic lifestyle.

Colorful, controversial, and stretching our understanding of what defined a beguine, the beata Sor María of Piedrahita[18] was an uneducated peasant woman who came to fame as a mystic, visionary, and reformer. Also known as María de Santo Domingo, she associated herself with assorted religious houses of Dominican women. She was quite passionate in preaching reform among these Dominican houses, and thus found herself needing to move on to other places at times. She lived a rather unorthodox lifestyle and dressed neither as a nun, beata, nor conventional Spanish woman; instead, she seemed to favor hats, skirts of fine scarlet cloth, and bracelets, and carried around a pouch of red satin containing relics of saints. Her defenders claimed that her flamboyant clothing expressed her humility, as she wore what she had been given and also in order for others to think lowly of her, while her opponents saw her as a self-serving fraud.

Born in the later 1400s to devout, illiterate laborers in a village near Ávila, little is known of Sor María's childhood. One village priest recalled that she fasted frequently and that her penances included self-flagellation (not an uncommon practice among penitents of her day). She confessed and received communion far more often than was common and gave alms to the poor even though she herself was destitute. At seventeen she became a lay Dominican in Piedrahita near Ávila. In 1504 she moved to the lay Dominican community of Santo Catalina and in 1507 to the community of Santo Tomás, both in Ávila. Later that year, Sor María, with a group of female and male followers, went to Toledo with the intent of reforming Dominican houses there.

At Toledo, Sor María's reform attempts were met with deep resistance. Her public raptures (which reportedly occurred when she received communion) were accompanied by prophecies that claimed divine authority for her attempts at reform; she also increasingly condemned various people. Her attire and behavior grew more and more colorful, and the number of both followers and detractors swelled.

Around 1518 Sor María's *Book of Prayer* was composed. It contains her sayings while she was (allegedly) in ecstasy, as well as dictations after her ecstatic experiences. The book is a carefully constructed literary and theological entity. For example, her "Contemplation While Enraptured on Easter Sunday" (which is considered dramatic literature) has three distinct parts, with opening and closing prayers that explicate the themes of sin, penitence, salvation, and faith. The cast of characters includes the Blessed Virgin, Mary of Magdala, the disciples John and Peter, as well as Sor María.

In her *Book of Prayer*, Sor María reaffirms a beguine spirituality.

God is love, and love is the ground of being, and life is about growing in love for and with God. She stands in the tradition of affective mystics seeking mystical union. She makes use of garden imagery, of hoeing and planting and fertilizing, and of musical imagery, especially that of the clavichord. For example, she sings, "Oh sweet and good Jesus, Who can know the disharmony of souls if not He Himself who in creating them knew how to tune them and knows how to play them? What sin put out of tune, Your blood tuned. For You know the harmony and disharmony of souls."[19]

Like Christina the Astonishing and Elizabeth of Spalbeek, Sor María reenacted Jesus's Passion, either in a chapel or in her room, at times becoming rigid in the form of a cross. She reenacted and sang the dialogue for each of the biblical characters. Surviving records indicate that Sor María's religious drama was witnessed by only a few people at a time, yet she enjoyed an extraordinary reputation. Her reenactments were deeply connected to her devotion to Jesus who suffered and was crucified. In one song she said, in the person of Jesus: "My blood will be shed for you so you may have a precious bath of charity in it and love in which to cleanse and wash yourselves. It is not that I am unable to rear you in grace and sustain you in grace without having to shed My blood, but it was necessary for your sake that I come down among you, become a man like you, and shed my blood for you so that my love [. . .] might raise you up more for me and make you more conformed to me and thus enhance your happiness with me."[20]

Sor María was deeply devoted to the eucharist, repeatedly claiming that she "saw" Jesus in the consecrated host. Witnesses claimed that she would often become enraptured at the moment of consecration even though she was in her cell at the time and not in the chapel. Sor María was also reportedly a stigmatic.

Witnesses claimed that she bore a wound in her right side that bled on occasion, and that the bleeding and corresponding pain were particularly acute on Good Friday of each year. She was also believed to have exercised the capacity to "read souls." In her case, this ability seemed to be directly connected with her reform efforts among the Dominicans. While she enjoyed a wide following, Sor María also angered people when she claimed to know that they must repent of sin.

Sor María was at times associated by her accusers with the *alumbrados*, relying upon the "inner light" of the Holy Spirit rather than on the church's sacraments and other external works of devotion. But even though she was brought to trial by the Inquisition in 1509/10, she was exonerated. Inquisitions were a long, drawn-out process. Men who testified in her case claimed that her theology had remained in accordance with the teachings of the church. She also benefitted from powerful supporters —King Ferdinand of Aragon; Francisco Ximénez de Cisneros, confessor to Queen Isabel and inquisitor general as of 1507; and Fernando Álvarez de Toledo, Duke of Alba. Thus the Inquisition could not harm her. Sor María remained a popular yet polarizing beata, spending her last years as prioress in Aldeanueva until her death around 1524.

The medieval world's rich imagination thrived on passionate preaching and religious drama and performance. Beguines were resourceful in capturing this imagination in order to convey their message in a way that both encouraged their audiences to accept God's love for them and challenged them to turn their lives around. While beguines may not have been preachers in the formal sense (compared to clerics authorized by religious authorities), they were preachers in the most authentic sense: they dwelt among the spiritually hungry and hurting.

8

LITERARY
BEGUINES

B EGUINES WERE NOT only effective preachers and performers, they also created outstanding texts: spiritual autobiographies, mystical treatises, and passionate letters of spiritual direction, spiritual consolation, or moral exhortation written to their friends and followers. Beguines also wrote poetry, some of which was set to music. Some of the beguines' literary texts were most likely polished summaries of years of teaching and preaching that allowed for wide dissemination across Europe.

Most beguines did not "write books" as we understand it today. A beguine's friends and followers might record some of her teachings and public preaching or preserve her letters. Some books were compiled after a beguine's death. And a number of the sacred texts we have from the beguines were carefully crafted as a partnership between the beguine and her spiritual director or confessor. The medieval world did not clearly differentiate between a text or book written by one person (such as Marguerite Porete and her *Mirror of Simple Souls*) versus dictated tracts, pieces of writing assembled by spiritual advisors or friends, or words taught or preached that were then written down by one of the listeners. But medieval people did differ between the ability to read and the ability to write; these were considered separate skills to be learned.

Beguines were in the business of book production, too, working as copyists in workshops and sometimes even owning those workshops. They copied and illuminated texts for customers and worked as miniaturists, which was the delicate and painstaking painting of very small pictures and portraits. Beguines acquired manuscripts—autobiographies and biographies, histories and writings by other women—with the intent of copying them and making copies available for purchase. Some beguines made their living as *notaria*, or scribes, for businesses and the aristocracy.

Before Gutenberg and the printing press, owning any book was a great luxury. What kinds of books—if they could afford them—did beguines own? We know only so much about their reading interests. They would have possessed the Bible, prayer books, and Psalters. We know that some beguines were well-versed in the writings of certain theologians (particularly Augustine of Hippo and Bernard of Clairvaux) and they freely translated theology and Scripture from Latin into their own languages; they also copied down their favorite homilies delivered by cleric friends and made these available to others. Beguine mystics might dictate their visionary experiences, along with their carefully rendered interpretations and other teachings, to their scribes (among whom were fellow beguines), and such texts might then be copied and distributed.

Unlike kings and popes, leading nobility and clergy, or wealthy monasteries, beguines did not possess large collections of books—

for obvious financial reasons and because they did not found their beguinages in order to last for centuries. The exceptions were a few of the court beguinages that began to build library collections for communal use in the fifteenth and sixteenth centuries. Many beguine convents, along with their books, disappeared within a generation or two. But beguine wills did record thoughtful consideration in passing books on to family, friends, and fellow beguines (Psalters were frequently mentioned in wills, with the owner bequeathing her beloved Psalter to someone important to her), and we do know that there was an exchange of books both within and among beguine communities.

For example, in 1439 the pinzochera Jacobella de Tostis (who belonged to a prominent Roman clan) sold a house to purchase a Psalter worth one hundred florins. This Psalter, along with two other books of prayer, was designated for use by her fellow pinzochere. Around 1500, a Flemish beguine stipulated in her will that her donation of books was to be maintained at the Ghent beguinage *Ter Hoyen*, but the beguines there were free to loan the books out. Around this same time, *Ter Hoyen* also received seventy books—a sizable collection—from the widow Elisabeth de Gruutere.[1]

Psalters were the most commonly owned and preserved books among beguines, and they were often used for private prayer. Psalters included the 150 psalms of the Bible as well as canticles, a liturgical calendar, and short selections from the Old and New Testaments, all arranged to fit a four-week cycle. Some Psalters were for daily use and some for holy days. Many Psalters included the Hours of the Virgin, several devotional texts commemorating (among other sacred events) the Nativity of Mary and the Annunciation and culminating in Mary's Assumption and Coronation in Heaven. Psalters also included the Office of the Dead (Vespers, Matins, and Lauds for the vigils before the funeral mass).

Medieval manuscript producers rarely signed their work. One of the few such names historians have located is that of the beguine Babekin Boems of Brugge who worked as a professional manuscript illuminator between 1459 and 1488.[2] Also in Brugge, in the late 1480s Grietkin Sceppers, an experienced woman miniaturist and a member of the local guild of St. John the Evangelist, visited the new Carmelite monastery of Sion to train the sisters there as miniaturists. One of the first printing presses in Italy was purchased in 1476 and operated by a group of nuns at San Jacopo di Ripoli in Florence.

The literary production of the beguines is part of the great Christian mystical writings of the Middle Ages. Frequently beguines took the framework and style of a known form of literature and created something refreshingly new. Major vernacular mystical texts of the thirteenth century were written by four beguines: Mechthild of Magdeburg, Beatrijs of Nazareth, Hadewijch, and Marguerite Porete.

Mechthild of Magdeburg was born in about 1210 near Magdeburg into a noble family of Saxony and most likely grew up at a small court. At the young age of twelve she experienced her first "greeting" from the Holy Spirit, which left a deep impression upon her. When she was around twenty-two, Mechthild decided to devote her life to God, becoming a beguine in Magdeburg and eventually serving as magistra. She continued to have visions, and only in her early forties did she reveal this to her friend and confessor, the Dominican Heinrich of Halle, who persuaded her to document it all. She spent years writing down the substance of her visions and spiritual learning, carefully shaping her words until she was satisfied. Heinrich of Halle served as a sounding board for her "received" teachings and only helped shape the wording of sections dealing with difficult theological concepts (most likely to keep her manuscript from being scrutinized by the Inquisition).

Mechthild's masterpiece, *The Flowing Light of the Godhead*, was written in a Low German dialect, copied on vellum, and disseminated among her followers and friends. It is comprised of seven "books" or parts that contain stunningly beautiful and provocative expressions of poetry and prose, monologue and dialogue—visions, letters, parables, reflections, allegories, prayers, criticism, and advice—to paint a portrait of Mechthild's inner journey toward God. She completed the first four books in her forties and the fifth and sixth books in her fifties and sixties. The seventh and last book was composed after about 1270, while she resided with the Cistercian nuns at Helfta (near Halle). She remained in Helfta until her death in the late 1200s and enjoyed a significant following by both women and men whom she called "friends of God."

Mechthild, like many women of her era who needed to establish their authority as author and preacher, began the first book of *The Flowing Light of the Godhead* with a conversation between herself and God:

> "Ah, Lord God, who made this book?"
> "I made it in my powerlessness, for I cannot
> restrain myself as to my gifts."
> "Well, then, Lord, what shall the title of the book be,
> which is to your glory alone?"
> "It shall be called a flowing light of my Godhead
> into all hearts that live free of hypocrisy."[3]

Applying a common defense tactic of her day, Mechthild undermined her detractors by pointing to God as the one who had "commanded" her, a mere woman, to write down God's words.

Thus any reader who wanted to argue with the book's content could take up that argument with God directly.

The Flowing Light of the Godhead weaves together three strands from Mechthild's own world: her familiarity with the culture of the land-owning nobility and courtly life with its unique literature; aspects of the urban subculture of the beguines and their spirituality; and her friendship with scholarly Dominican friars. Mechthild also knew the Jewish community in Magdeburg and Jewish mystical teachings about the feminine face of God in exile (called *Shekhinah*).[4]

Mechthild portrays God through rich allegories: God is "triune," "flowing," and "pulsing with erotic love for his creatures." God is Love and Love bursts forth in paradox; Love is fiery and cool, merciful yet tormenting. God's relationship to the world is likened to a noble court, a self-contained sphere, a wine cellar, a stringed instrument, a crossbow, and a tree.[5] The seeker's relationship with God is expressed in terms of ecstasy and agony, God's presence and absence, and yet Mechthild insists that the seeker is in union with God even when unaware of God's immanence.

In her writings Mechthild utilizes common imagery found in the courtly love literature and storytelling culture of her day, including the soul as bride and Christ the bridegroom, the soul's journey to the court of God, and the hunt. Expressing the soul's yearning for God she writes:

> Ah dearest Love, for how long
> Hast thou lain in wait for me!
> What, O what can I do?
> I am hunted, captured, bound,
> Wounded so terribly
> That never can I be healed.

Cunning blows hast thou dealt,
Shall I ever recover from thee?
Would it not have been well
That I had never known thee?[6]

In her continued attempts to convey her hunger for the Divine, Mechthild speaks of a restlessness that she attributes to anything and everything not of God, which then leads to grief.

Mechthild intended her followers to prayerfully ponder, study, and discuss her words in the tradition of lectio divina. She knew that only in engaging and debating and discussing the text would her followers integrate her teachings into their lives. She wrote: "Do you want to know how you can best use God's holy favor and enjoy it as He wants you to? You know God's Will will teach you this itself, if you welcome it. Receive God's kindness externally (via virtues) and internally (through your yearnings). Respect it humbly. Never let go of it. Be submissive when things go wrong in your life. Give God's kindness time and room in you. That's all it asks. Then it will melt you so deeply into God, you will know what God's will is: You'll understand how long you should look for His intense caresses, and you'll know how and when to act kindly to your neighbors."[7] Mechthild was encouraging her followers to trust their relationship with God who desires to teach and shape each person. Like her fellow beguines, she insisted that even the lowliest member of society could have a personal and intimate relationship with God.

Mechthild was outspoken in her criticism of corruption within the church, and she stated, "I, poor woman, was so bold in my prayer that I impudently took corrupt Christianity into the arms of my soul and lifted it in lamentation."[8] It was said that in one vision she heard God say to the pope, "He who does not know the path to hell, let him look at the corrupt clergy."[9]

When challenged by such corrupt clergy, Mechthild claimed God as her authority for writing. On numerous occasions she was threatened with the burning of her work, and she told her followers that as she was facing this threat, God consoled her by reminding her that the truth cannot be burned by anyone, for no human is stronger than God. She said that God had stated that "the highest mountain cannot receive the revelation of My grace, for the flood of My Holy Spirit flows by nature into the valley. You find many a wise master, learned in the scripture who himself is a fool in My eyes."[10] Mechthild not only claimed God as her authority and as the one who had "ordered" her to write this book, but she expressed that it was God's intent that the lowliest of God's creatures be the author of these words.

In a synod held at Magdeburg in 1261, Archbishop Rupert of Magdeburg revoked the right of local beguines to self-governance, their relationship with the Dominicans was suppressed, and the women were placed under the authority of local clergy. This series of changes did not go over well with the beguines, and Mechthild became increasingly critical of the institutional church.

In *The Flowing Light of the Godhead*, Mechthild claimed that "God calls the cathedral clergy goats because their flesh stinks of impurity with regard to eternal truth, before His Holy Trinity ..." and she went on: "Alas! Crown of holy Church, how tarnished you have become. Your precious stones have fallen from you because you are weak and you disgrace the holy Christian faith. Your gold is sullied in the filth of unchastity, for you have become destitute and do not have true love. Your purity is burned up in the ravenous fire of gluttony; your humility has sunk to the swamp of your flesh; your truth has been destroyed in the lie of this world; the flowers of all your virtues have fallen from you. Alas, crown of holy priesthood, you have disappeared, and you have nothing left but your external shape—namely, priestly power—with this you do battle against God and His chosen friends. Therefore God will humble you before you know what has happened."[11] Mechthild had taken on her detractors and fought back.

With harsh words like these, she made enemies as well as friends and followers. Toward the end of her life, an elderly and nearly blind Mechthild left the beguine community with which she had long been associated and sought refuge in the Cistercian community of Helfta. There she significantly influenced the spiritual formation of the Helfta mystics Gertrude the Great (1256–c. 1301) and Mechthild of Hackeborn (1240–1298).

Although Beatrijs of Nazareth spent much of her adult life in a Cistercian monastery, she is often grouped together with Mechthild, Hadewijch, and Marguerite Porete. Considered an outstanding intellectual and artist, Beatrijs (who is also known as Beatrijs of Tienen) had been educated by beguines who had been important to her early spiritual formation, and she maintained a lifelong friendship with beguines.

Born in the town of Tienen (near Leuven) in 1200, Beatrijs was taught to read, along with the basics of grammar, by her mother. After her mother died around 1206, the girl was sent to the beguines at Léau to continue her education. Around 1210 Beatrijs became an oblate of the Cistercian community of Bloemendaal (Florival), which her father, Barthelmy De Vleeschouwer, a wealthy and devout merchant, had founded. (He later also founded the Cistercian houses of Maagdendaal, near Tienen, and Nazareth, near Antwerp.) Beatrijs loved this way of life and sought to become a novice at fifteen, making formal profession in 1216. She was sent to La Ramée (near Nivelles) to learn the art of copying and illuminating manuscripts.

Here she developed a strong friendship with Ida of Nivelles and also continued her education with several university-educated magisters. She spent some more time at Bloemendaal, then went to Maagdendaal (Val-des-Vierges), and moved to the newly founded convent of Nazareth in 1236. She served as prioress there until her death in 1268.

We have only one short prose work by Beatrijs, *The Seven Manners of Loving,*[12] which was the product of years of prayerful reflection on her powerful experience of God. The seven manners are not presented as steps in an ascending order, but rather as different ways of experiencing *minne* (love presented as a person). Beatrijs begins with the words "There are seven manners of loving, which come out of the highest and return to the most high."[13]

Beatrijs speaks of the first manner of loving as an active desire to restore one's soul into the image of God, in whose image the soul was created. This desire impels one to the hard work of growing in self-knowledge, in virtues, and thus knowledge of God. Beatrijs notes that this desire is motivated by love and not fear.

The soul has a second manner of loving when at times it offers itself to God to serve God with no expectation of return, making this offer only in love and asking for no answer, no reward of grace or of glory. The soul simply longs to serve God (Love). In this manner the soul burns with desire for God and is willing to suffer joyfully on behalf of God.

Beatrijs's third manner of loving is realizing and accepting the radical nature of faith—that believing and trusting in God may not necessarily mean experiencing God as we would wish. This strong desire for deeper faith may involve feeling frustrated in any attempts at attaining it. This lack of deeper faith or a more meaningful experience of God results in suffering as the soul longs to be sufficient for God (Love). Yet this mature love (on our part) can endure all things and grow in mature wholeness through all that life hands us.

Her fourth manner of loving is an infusion of abundant divine love. The soul is so delighted with God's immediate presence and so absorbed in love that it seems to be love itself. Beatrijs describes one's heart "touched tenderly by love and eagerly drawn into love and passionately affected by love and violently overwhelmed by love and lovingly embraced in love, so that she [one's soul] is altogether conquered by love."[14] Beatrijs goes on to describe that "she [one's soul] feels herself to be in the overflowing of rapture and in the great fullness of the heart, her spirit sinks wholly into love and her body escapes her, her heart melts and all her strength is lost. She is so conquered by love that she is hardly in possession of herself and often loses control over all her members and her senses."[15] This experience of overpowering love seems to leave the seeker without any sense of a body.

The fifth manner of loving is when love is powerfully strengthened and rises up violently—a "stormy love" or "love's tempest"—with great tumult and force, as if it would break the heart with its assault and drag the soul out of itself in the exercise and the delight of love. The soul is drawn by the longing of love to fulfill the great and pure deeds of love and the desires implanted by love's many promptings. Beatrijs writes that "love awakens in the soul, stormily rises with great tempestuousness and fierce passion, as if with its rage it would break the heart and tear the soul out of herself and beyond herself. Love becomes so boundless and so overflowing in the soul—when love strongly and fiercely stirs inside her—that it seems to her as if her heart is badly wounded again and again and that daily her wounds are renewed and intensified with ever more and new pain."[16]

In her sixth manner of loving, love has conquered the soul's every shortcoming and has mastered the senses and adorned the soul's humanity, and increased and exalted the soul's being, utterly overpowering the soul's being without any resistance. Thus the soul is made steadfast in confidence and can freely practice all the exercises of love, and delight in love, and take its rest in love—in other words, the soul is experiencing pure divine love.

In Beatrijs's seventh manner of loving, the soul is wholly immersed in love, which is eternal love beyond human understanding, beyond time and space. Beatrijs describes this love as love lived within the Trinity—or the limitless abyss of Divinity.[17]

Beatrijs's spirituality was influenced by both courtly love and by the writings of Bernard of Clairvaux. Yet her words became suspicious to the Inquisition: here was a woman writing upon her own authority, a woman testifying to a direct experience of God, and reflecting on "soul" without gender, thereby suggesting that women were equal to men in the eyes of God. Scholars believe that followers of Beatrijs burned her original manuscript for protection from the Inquisition and that copies that had been created were hidden.

We have a significant body of texts by the Flemish beguine Hadewijch, yet we know little about her life. Hadewijch was a common medieval name and little evidence exists that this great poet and mystic enjoyed fame while she lived. Her extensive writings—thirty-one letters, forty-five poems in stanzas, fourteen visions, and sixteen poems in couplets—were preserved in the fourteenth century in two monastic communities. She was then "rediscovered" in the 1800s. Her writings are now considered among the masterpieces of Low Countries literature.

Hadewijch was a beguine living in the thirteenth century—

perhaps connected to Antwerp or Brussels—whose familiarity with the vocabulary of chivalry and courtly love suggests that she came from an aristocratic background. She may even have been a musician or troubadour before becoming a beguine. She knew Latin and French as well as the writings of Origen, Augustine of Hippo, Bernard of Clairvaux, William of St. Thierry, and Richard of St. Victor. Hadewijch's writings frequently allude to biblical Scripture with impressive precision. Her choice of writing in Middle Dutch (rather than Latin), of which she had a voracious command, showed her intent on reaching a wide readership among the laity, especially among her fellow beguines.

Hadewijch is considered one of the most exquisite and exacting creators of the courtly love poetry so valued in her day—and she crafted her poetry as an expression of longing for God. As we have seen, courtly love poetry favored images of the unattainable lover, the submissive service to love, the complaints, the hope and despair, and the all-pervading power of love.[18] While these courtly poems contain stories of star-crossed lovers and the gentleman suitor searching for the unattainable lady, Hadewijch's mystical poetry centered on the sense of agony that the unceasing desire for oneness with God caused in her—a woman seeking the Beloved and the Beloved seeking her.

Hadewijch was apparently involved in the spiritual formation of beguines. Most of her letters were written for beguines and exhorted them to a deeper, loving inner life, and ultimately to self-awareness—"understand the deepest essence of your soul."[19] In one letter she told her reader, "with the Humanity of God you must live here on earth, in the labors and sorrows of exile, while within your soul you love and rejoice for the truth of both the Humanity and the divinity is one single fruition."[20] Her writings reveal a very passionate life that was never sentimental or childish; her pursuit of God was that of a mature person.

While she was adamant that young beguines should acquire an excellent education, Hadewijch insisted on the primacy of love over reason and intellect, explaining to fellow beguines that intellectual pursuits could only speak of what God is *not*. Love, the meeting of the human and the Divine, for her was an embodied experience. Hadewijch set a high standard for cultivating such a rich inner life; nothing was as important to her as this inner pilgrimage to God.

Hadewijch insisted that love renews and rejuvenates our souls when we seek God's presence. A clear indicator for her that the seeker was honestly attempting the spiritual journey was a sense of "newness" each day. In one of her poems Hadewijch wrote:

> Love is always new!
> Those who live in Love,
> are renewed each day
> and through their frequent acts of goodness
> are born all over again.

> How can anyone stay old in Love's presence?
> How can anyone be timid there?

> Mature souls always have new wisdom.
> They never hesitate to give themselves away to Love
> in every new moment.
> I call these old people the Rejuvenated.

> They become attached to Love.
> They look on Love with passion always,
> and live.[21]

Hadewijch's writings reveal her strong belief in the importance of community, and of relationships within community. She expressed this necessity through her teachings of the meaning of the Holy Trinity and of our relationship to the human Jesus and the divine Christ. It is believed that she was evicted from her beguinage and forced into exile, and thus Hadewijch may have come to recognize the importance of what had been taken from her.

Literary texts accredited to beguines were preserved, copied, and disseminated over the centuries, often by monastery and university libraries. The varied styles of writing utilized by beguines to engage, educate, and encourage their followers continued to attract readers. In the twentieth century a surge in research regarding beguine writings began, enlivened by modern women seeking to reclaim their spiritual history. Contemporary seekers look to these texts for inspiration, and monastics read them during the Divine Office.

9

WERE BEGUINES
HERETICS?

THE INQUISITION SENTENCED the *"beguine clergesse"* Marguerite Porete, a learned beguine preacher and writer, to be burned at the stake as a relapsed heretic at the Place de Grève in Paris. Her execution took place on June 1, 1310. Her crime was a daring work of mystical theology called *The Mirror of Simple Souls*, which she had composed in Old French and shared with others.

We know little about Marguerite's life. She probably came from the region of Hainaut in the Low Countries, and she was brave, outspoken, and critical of the church hierarchy. She had been pursued by the Inquisition for some years before her death. Although three theologians (the friar John of Querayn, the Cistercian monk François de Villiers, and the master of theology Godfrey of Fontaines) approved of *The Mirror*, Marguerite, unlike other beguines who preached and wrote, apparently lacked a powerful male defender. The bishop of Cambrai, who had jurisdiction over Hainaut, had publicly burned an early copy of *The Mirror* sometime between 1296 and 1306 and had ordered Marguerite to cease disseminating her teachings—but she continued undeterred. In fact, she added several more chapters and a prologue to her book and continued to circulate it (even sending it to a bishop), and she also kept preaching. But the odds were against her.

Marguerite was arrested and jailed in 1308 on the order of the Dominican inquisitor William of Paris, who had also served as confessor to the French king Philip IV (1268–1314). During her imprisonment and questioning over many months, she remained silent and refused to answer her accusers. (Her refusal to cooperate with authorities was perhaps motivated in part because she considered herself a citizen of the German empire, yet it was the French who had arrested her.[1])

Marguerite had the bad fortune of living at a time when both the French king and the church in Rome were aggressively attempting to stamp out what they saw as heresy. (In order to suppress heresy, the papacy had set up the apparatus of the Inquisition in the 1200s.) She was condemned both for suggesting that the church and its sacraments may not be necessary for salvation and for defying church authorities. She was probably also a political victim of the witch hunt launched by King Philip against the Templars in 1307, although no inquisitor accused her of being either a Knight Templar or a sympathizer. The church was also gearing up for the Council of Vienne (1311–12, near Lyon) that attempted to suppress not only the Templars but also the beguine way of life. Theologians preparing their cases for the condemnation of all beguines, along with certain emerging spiritual movements (such as the Spiritual Franciscans), took a keen interest in Marguerite's case—as justification for why their orthodox position should prevail.

In *The Mirror of Simple Souls*, Marguerite Porete attempts to express her understanding of the soul's relationship with the Divine, especially the nature of the soul's freedom and its potential perfectibility. She understands a person's soul as having the capacity to draw so close to God—even here on earth and in this life—that literally nothing stands between the soul and God: not reason, virtue, good works, or even the sacraments. Marguerite is not condemning any of the above things, but is saying that we can sufficiently mature in our relationship to God so that we can leave behind the need for these things.

Marguerite's writings implied that the church as provider of the sacraments and guarantor of salvation was not essential to a person's relationship with God; while the church could be important for people's spiritual health, it was possible for a person to grow spiritually so mature that the church's sacraments were no longer necessary nor even essential for that person. She taught that Reason is below Love, since Reason cannot understand Love's teachings. *The Mirror of Simple Souls* includes dialogues between the characters Soul, Love, and Reason, and Love alone is shown to be the proper relationship between the human and the Divine—a relationship that propels the soul toward God.

Marguerite speaks of the soul's "deaths," which transition or propel the soul toward maturity and perfection (wholeness): "You, soul, have known the divine touch, been set apart from sin in the first stage of grace; may divine grace lead you to the seventh stage, in which the soul reaches the fullness of perfection in the peace of the love of God."[2] The first "death" is when a person so cultivates a virtuous life that they can live without attachment: neither wealth, nor honor, nor reputation have a hold on them. Finally there is the "death" of the spirit, meaning the seeker has moved beyond their personal will—which in Marguerite's understanding is a barrier between the seeker and God—into perfect "annihilation" where the only will is the will of love, the divine will. "In this state of annihilation the soul finds her perfection; she no longer has a will with which to will or desire, but rather God's will alone wills in her."[3]

The Mirror of Simple Souls reveals Marguerite's familiarity with the writings of Augustine of Hippo, Bernard of Clairvaux, Bonaventure, Richard of St. Victor, and William of St. Thierry. She also uses familiar themes from courtly love poetry to express her spiritual understandings. One of her significant influences was to confront the church with its dualistic divisions of culture and theology, suggesting a resolution in the life of the mystic. Her life was a powerful reminder to the church that contemplation and active ministry could be natural companions—an insight Marguerite shared with her fellow beguines.

Despite being condemned, *The Mirror of Simple Souls* survived and continued to be read. Some theologians and writers copied sections and integrated them into their own works. The Dominican Meister Eckhart (c. 1260–c. 1327) knew Marguerite's work and he, too, lived under the suspicion of heresy. The Flemish theologian and mystic Jan van Ruysbroeck (1293–1381) also knew *The Mirror*. Monasteries preserved copies of Marguerite's work and translated it into other languages, including English and Italian. Often *The Mirror* was circulated as an anonymous work, and as such it became eventually absorbed into the canon of Christian theology.

A heretic is a person who allegedly corrupts established faith doctrine, often by selecting a limited set of beliefs and denying the other parts of orthodox teaching. In the highly charged political environment of the medieval world, both secular and clerical leaders at times presumed that their political positions were equal to church dogma. Rarely did a beguine's teachings fail to meet the standards of church dogma. However, in a society strongly defined by each person's specific place (such as belonging to the guilds or merchants, to aristocratic or religious classes, or to the peasantry), beguines were violating their "God-assigned place" in order to serve the gospel. As we have seen, beguines were smart and savvy businesswomen who angered the guilds by using their competitive edge in business. These women owned houses, farms, and land—and greedy neighbors, both secular and religious, often tried to take over such beguine properties. The beguines did not acquiesce but fought back through their political astuteness in order to protect their financial interests, thus possibly setting off fabricated charges of heresy.

But primarily beguines were under church investigation at different times and in different parts of Europe for their spiritual independence. The powerful always attempt to control God— and the Christian aspect of God that is perhaps most "uncontrollable" is the Holy Spirit. A few preaching beguines did place such emphasis on the Holy Spirit that they essentially negated the need for the church and its sacraments. Ultimately, the authorities—power-driven and often misogynist men—could not tolerate women who were speaking of their own (intimate) experience of God and proving to be such effective competitors in the realm of the spiritual.

Most beguines under investigation for heresy were blamed for their preaching and teaching (especially when the topic was the Trinity), even when their words were well within church tradition. They were also accused of heresy because of certain individuals with whom they associated, usually preachers of apocalyptic messages. Apocalyptic preaching—declaring that the end times were drawing near—could create economic havoc, since believers of such messages might well abandon their farms and businesses in order to prepare for the end. Not surprisingly, some of these charismatic (itinerant) preachers were suspected of heresy.

Another motivation for church authorities to rein in beguines was connected to celibacy. While celibacy for monastics was well-established by the High Middle Ages, the church was attempting to enforce celibacy for its parish clergy as well. But often when clerics were found to behave immorally, a woman was to be blamed—and since beguines lived independently, they were readily accused as seductresses of "innocent" clerics. The church felt that controlling such independent women would help it to enforce the celibacy of priests.

Lastly, a key concern of the church seems to have been the strong influence that beguines exercised among the laity as a result of the powerful tool of interdict. As mentioned, when interdict was forced onto a region, the celebration of mass was forbidden, access to sacraments was denied, and oftentimes the Divine Office had to be recited quietly rather than being chanted. Denial of both the last rites and burial in consecrated ground was a cruel interdict tactic, since the average Christian feared that not having either might condemn them to eternal hell.

Countless times in the Middle Ages, secular and religious leaders clashed over whose authority would reign supreme when conflicts between church and state arose. While kings and princes had their armies to defend their position, popes and bishops controlled access to the sacraments—and therefore access to God—and thus employed the powerful weapon of interdict in their battles against secular authorities. Interdict, which could last for years or even decades, terrorized the innocent: the common believer was caught in the middle of an ongoing power fight whose outcome was never beneficial to the layperson.

From the eleventh through the thirteenth centuries, interdict was imposed frequently and broadly against different realms and regions because of the battles between church and state. And inadvertently, the repetitive imposing of interdict encouraged beguines to exercise the pastoral ministry that the official church was withholding: preaching and teaching and leading informal prayer gatherings. Beguines filled the spiritual void created by an order of interdict, and thus their popularity grew. Consequently, churchmen felt that their authority was being undermined and they tried to silence all unauthorized preachers and worship practices.

Pope Innocent III convened the Fourth Lateran Council in 1215 in Rome, a great assembly of hundreds of bishops, abbots, and worldly representatives with a long list of agenda items. The Council declared that no new religious orders were permitted; orders "that have not obtained papal confirmation are forever prohibited and quashed, no matter how far they have progressed."[4] But were the beguines exempt from this announcement since they were not a religious order? This detail was one of the questions theologians were debating at the Council.

As we have seen, certain bishops wanted to protect beguines because these women filled a vital social need in their dioceses and because they had many supporters among the laity. Jacques de Vitry, as cardinal, campaigned on behalf of the beguines, winning them certain protections from Pope Honorius III. However, not all bishops or theologians recognized this protection, seeking to either force beguines into monasteries or disperse the women while confiscating their property.

Beguines had to endure public mockery from their detractors. One of those was the French poet Rutebeuf in the later 1200s, who vilified and satirized the beguines in a number of his works. In one text he sarcastically claimed that "whatever happens in her [the beguine's] life is religious in character; her word is prophecy; if she laughs it is good manners; if she weeps it is devotion; if she sleeps she is in ecstasy; if she dreams it is a vision; if she lies think nothing of it; if she marries it is because she is sociable; her vows and profession are not for life; last year she wept; this year she prays; next year she will take a husband; now she is Martha, now Mary."[5] Another opponent was the French philosopher and satirist William of Saint-Amour (c. 1200–1272), who hammered incessant accusations of hypocrisy against the beguines, claiming that they dazzled by false affectation of holiness and followed none of the austerities of religious life. Ultimately, he was railing against the beguines because of the large number of converts and followers they had gained, fearing that these women were "competing" with clergymen. He insisted they either give up their way of life or be excommunicated.

Conrad of Marburg (c. 1180–1233), a papal inquisitor in Germany, actively pursued alleged heretics, including beguines, in Flanders, France, and the Rhineland. The Dominican Robert le Bourge[6] was also ruthless in his pursuit of alleged heretics, persecuting them in Champagne and Flanders between 1233 and 1239. In Douai and Lille alone he had about thirty people executed, earning him the nickname "Robert the Damned." In Cambrai in 1236 he ordered the execution of the beguine Aeleis for heresy. Hadewijch proclaimed that Aeleis had died for "her righteous love."

Pope Gregory X convened a council (called the Second Council of Lyon) in 1274. While a possible reunion of the Western and Eastern churches was at the core of this gathering, beguines also received attention. In preparation for this Council, the Franciscan Guibert of Tournai wrote a document called *On the Scandals of the Church* and made a rather biting comment about the beguines in it: "There are in our lands women called beguines, some of whom are famous for their subtleties and enjoy speculating about novelties. They have interpreted the mysteries of Scripture and translated them in the common vernacular, although even the best experts in Scripture can hardly comprehend them. They read these texts together, without due respect, boldly, in their little convents and in their workshops, or even in public places."[7] Guibert was mocking the beguines for translating the Scriptures on their own accord into their native tongues and making these sacred texts available to laypeople.

The Synod of Liège in 1287 forbade any woman who did not live in a beguinage to wear the distinctive garb of a beguine or to share in the respect extended to beguines. The Synod also prohibited any woman whose business earned more than ten marks per year from wearing the distinctive beguine garb and enjoying respect accordingly—the guilds' resentments might have influenced this ruling. In the year 1290, beguines in Colmar (Alsace) and Basel (Switzerland) were arrested for heresy. The beguine Katherina was driven from Mainz in 1296 because she lived on her own and was thus suspected of teaching heresy. Beguines living independent lives, oftentimes preaching and teaching, were particular targets of the inquisitors.

In 1298, Pope Boniface VIII issued the papal bull *Periculoso*, which mandated enclosure for all religious women. While beguines felt some social pressure to conform, they variably interpreted this bull according to their own standards. In Umbria, the bull actually stimulated the founding and growth of bizzoche communities,[8] since some penitential women's communities adopted Franciscan Third Order rules in order to protect themselves from enforced enclosure.

But the pressure put on the papacy from theologians and guilds to fully suppress all beguines (and to seize their properties) kept rising. As mentioned, one of the agenda items for the Council of Vienne was the beguines. A year earlier, Marguerite

Porete had been burned at the stake, and six of her theologian accusers were in Vienne. These men inferred a connection between her ideas and beguines in general. The Council officially condemned beguines, but primarily this was directed at wandering beguines who were not living in court beguinages or convents and were not under the supervision of male officials. The Council issued the decree *Ad Nostrum Qui*, listing eight errors ascribed to the beguines. The main concern was specific beguine teachings that claimed some beguines had attained such a degree of perfection and spirit of freedom that they were no longer capable of sinning and therefore not subject to the church or in fact any human authority. The Council also condemned beguines for translating and debating Scripture.

Because the Inquisition kept detailed records, we have some related knowledge about individual beguines and their communities. While most beguines were quite orthodox, there were some religious laywomen who did join the Cathars, the Free Spirits, the Spiritual Franciscans, and other suspected heretical movements. Laywomen in southern France who were suspected of participating in heretical movements were usually called "beguins."

The belief system of the Cathars was dualistic: the body was suspect and evil, while thoughts and spirit were without blemish, thus divine. Cathars believed the physical world was the creation of an evil demon, most fully embodied in a woman's capacity to bear children. Beguines, on the other hand, defended the created world, including the human body with its emotions and passions, as being in the image of a loving Creator.

The Spiritual Franciscans, followers of the Franciscan Peter John Olivi (c. 1248–1298), advocated a strict and abject poverty, condemned the church for abandoning the gospel in favor of wealth and power, and claimed to know the exact day and time of Jesus's return. Pope John XXII in 1323 declared the Spiritual Franciscans' teaching on apostolic poverty to be a formal heresy, which intensified the prosecution of these men and their laywomen friends. Between 1318 and 1330, some of Olivi's followers in Languedoc and Provence were burned for their beliefs.

A well-known woman mystic and beguin was Na Prous Boneta; she was burned at the stake in 1325. Our only record of her is her statement to the Inquisition in Montpellier shortly before her death. She and her sister Alisette lived in Montpellier among fellow beguins and Spiritual Franciscans, where she was a quiet but strong leader in the group. Na Prous was arrested and imprisoned in 1315 and later released. She might have witnessed the burning of beguins at Narbonne in 1317 and that of four Spiritual Franciscans the following year in Marseille.

In 1320 Na Prous began having visions. On Good Friday, 1321, while she was at the Franciscan church at Montpellier contemplating the Passion of Christ, she "felt herself to be transported into the first Heaven, where she encountered Jesus Christ, both in the form of a man and in his divinity. He showed her his heart, which she saw was pierced with holes like a lantern, and streaming with light like the sun. He gave her his heart in spirit. In vain, she protested that she was unworthy of such an honor; for Christ responded that he would do even more for her if she would be faithful to him. Coming close to him, she placed her head on his body, and saw nothing other than the light streaming from Christ himself. Weeping and sobbing, in the greatest fervor and love for God, she found herself placed gently back in her seat in church."[9]

These visions continued and her stature as a leader among the Montpellier beguins grew. Na Prous came to believe that she was the herald of a new age and that, in some way, she *was* the Holy Spirit. Because of the church's persecutions and book burnings, Na Prous came to declare that its sacraments were no longer valid and that the pope was the Antichrist. In her testimony to the Inquisition she stated that "every day and night and every hour she [Na Prous] sees God in the spirit, and he never leaves her; she says that Christ himself wishes to be head of the church and to guide souls, and that now he shall not permit souls to be ruled by any pope, even if another be elected by the cardinals, since the papacy is annulled for perpetuity. When questioned as to what way God rules souls, she said that by the Holy Spirit he does this."[10] Her condemnation of the sacraments and her belief that she was the third person of the Trinity, as well as her challenging of the authority of bishops and popes and the wealth of rulers and the church, could not be tolerated by the authorities. Na Prous Boneta had to die.

The Spanish Inquisition was set up by the Catholic Monarchs, Ferdinand and Isabella, in the late 1400s. Although we have lost most of the writings of the Spanish beatas to the inquisitors' fires, we do have historical records of their lives because of the Inquisition's scrupulous recordkeeping.

The Inquisition pursued beatas with charges of heresy, usually for "leading ecstatic prayer meetings" or "religious enthusiasm," for claiming ecstatic visions, for allegedly using "strange powers to heal and prophesy," and for heretical teaching. With rare exceptions, the charge of heretical teaching simply meant that a beata taught and preached publicly, and as a woman her teachings must therefore be filled with error. Inquisition records reveal that a major area of concern was the popularity and power of beatas versus church authorities. While a few women were executed, such as María de Borborques in 1559, most beatas were publicly forced to do penance and to live henceforth in seclusion in cloistered convents.

But the Inquisition investigated beatas primarily for their independence. Spanish rulers were attempting to control all women, sequestering them to homes and monasteries, and beatas in public ministry made these powerful men uncomfortable. On the other hand, ministry contained within a monastery was acceptable, as was a holy woman visiting prisons with a male chaperone (either a family member or a member of a religious community). When beatas resisted such control they were accused of heresy, put on trial, and condemned to a convent. Only powerful or cunning beatas could outwit the Inquisition.

Spanish authorities in the 1500s and 1600s were also uncomfortable with a popular and informal spiritual movement known as *alumbradismo* (meaning, enlightened), a mystical expression of Christianity that stressed inner illumination by the Holy Spirit. At its most extreme, such a spirituality would deny the importance of worship, the sacraments, Scripture, and even society itself. A person with a deep devotion to trusting what they considered the leading of the Holy Spirit would have been referred to as an *alumbrado*. Church authorities were skeptical of the increasing preference for individualistic prayer and anything that might signal a rejection of papal authority, usually in the form of lack of obedience to the local bishop, or any sense of disparagement of the sacraments. These tendencies were deemed a threat to society and church.

Because sixteenth-century Spanish society considered it a religious virtue for women to withdraw from the public sphere and to deny their own experience, inner authority, and power,[11] the autonomy of beatas was increasingly seen as a lack of allegiance to the institutional church. Church authorities began expressing concern with beatas moving freely about cities and towns, ministering to the poor, and enjoying more spiritual authority than most clerics. These women were getting caught between a male-formulated ideal of "womanhood" behind walls and grilles and the realities of social disintegration that came with the brutality of wars and colonization. Beatas were attempting to minimize the harm done to the vulnerable members of society, and they were punished for it.

Francisca Hernández was born in the later 1400s in Canella near Salamanca to a simple family. She showed unusual spiritual virtues from an early age, but because she could not afford a monastic dowry or a proper education she was unable to enter religious life. Instead she lived as a beata. The Inquisition in Salamanca began an investigation into this charismatic woman who enjoyed the comforts of life offered her by followers as well as the company of male friends. In 1519, when she learned that formal charges were pending, Francisca moved to Valladolid where her status, both good and bad, continued to grow. No doubt her comfort in the company of men left her with a reputation for promiscuity. Her popularity was largely due to a spirituality that encouraged her followers to nourish a personal relationship with God through prayer and immersion in Scripture rather than through external practices and adherence to church dogma.[12] Her spiritual counsel relieved some who sought her help in their struggles with excessive scrupulosity. She was frequently consulted on her interpretation of certain passages of Scripture and she taught her followers that creation, including sensuality, was good and not to be disdained.

While alumbradismo tendencies lurked about Francisca's spiritual teachings, it was ultimately her independent lifestyle that, in 1529, led to her arrest and imprisonment in Toledo. When members of her inner circle publicly defended her, they, too, were arrested and even tortured. After a number of trials based on testimony secured under torture and threats of torture, Francisca's case was settled by placing her into a house of beatas under the protection of the Benedictines. There she disappeared from further records.

Francisca de los Apóstoles (c. 1539–after 1578) was a beata in Toledo known for her visions and call for reform. At sixteen she left her parents' home to live as a beata at a local church until, after eight years, she moved to a church in Toledo. She established a beaterio, even though she had not received permission from church authorities to do so, and thus began her antagonistic relationship with the church. Toledo faced major social upheaval and great poverty at the time, and Francisca and her fellow beatas taught skills to marginal women so that they could support themselves and avoid sliding into prostitution. She again sought formal permission to establish houses with some degree of enclosure for poor women, but the permission never came.

In a series of visions that Francisca apparently received during the year 1574, God told her of all the offenses that humanity committed against God. These visions also showed her the final judgment day that attacked the corruption in the church. Not surprisingly, Francisca's visions were a challenge to the church of Toledo, which was not interested in reforming its corrupt ways. The more Francisca claimed that her visions were from God, the more she was scrutinized by civil and religious authorities. In a letter to her sister, Francisca wrote: "Times are so hard that my heart aches because of the tremendous necessity here in Toledo."[13]

Francisca was popular in Toledo, with a reputation as a woman of prayer who had access to divine wisdom and spiritual power. The Inquisition could not charge Francisca with heresy, but it needed to discredit her visions. She was condemned in 1578 for "false religious experiences" and also, of course, for sexual promiscuity. She received one hundred lashes and was then banished from Toledo.

There are other examples of Spanish women attempting to

live independently. The beata Catalina de Cardona, a friend of Teresa of Ávila, lived in a cave near Ávila for eight years where she met with her students and offered spiritual direction. Catalina refused every attempt by the Inquisition to force her into a cloistered monastery, as she did not want to be cut off from contact with ordinary people. Even though investigated by the Inquisition for her "pride," Catalina refused to take orders from the church.

In Toledo, the beata Francisca de Ávila, another contemporary of Teresa of Ávila, established a beaterio for poor young women. She reportedly received visions, offered spiritual counsel, and pressed for church reform regarding women. She was condemned by the Inquisition in 1578 for her independence.

Madre Catalina de Jesús (c. 1565–after 1633)[14] became the most celebrated beata facing the Inquisition in Seville. She preached and taught, prophesied and wrote. (Unfortunately, none of her writings, some of which were published in her day and most likely confiscated by the Inquisition, have so far been located by scholars.) Madre Catalina was known to have many male followers, including clerics. As with other beguines, her alleged gift of prophecy included the ability to "read souls." While her followers considered her to be the successor to Teresa of Ávila, her detractors accused her of being an alumbrado. The first round of accusations against her occurred in 1612 and ended with a suspended case. A second round of accusations and investigation resumed in 1622. Madre Catalina endured public penance in 1627 and was condemned to six years of seclusion.

Were beguines heretics? Most of them were not, but some were. The preaching and teaching of beguines mostly fell within the norms of orthodox medieval theology. Beguines rarely raised issues that were not already being explored and debated by male theologians. The emphasis that beguines placed on a loving God and on a deeper prayer life and their descriptions of purgatory, for example, raised little concern among the powerful. But as we have seen, beguine preaching on the Trinity did raise concern among theologians. Sometimes, as with the beguin Na Prous Boneta, a woman's spiritual message was sliding into the realm of heterodoxy or outright heresy. History does record a few beguines who went to the extreme of denying the reality of sin or of claiming to be God and/or the Holy Spirit.

Most charges of heresy, however, were politically motivated. When beguines challenged inept clergy, they made priests and bishops angry. When beguines condemned the greed and corruption within the church, they made the church hierarchy angry. When beguines denounced the cruelty done to innocent laypeople through interdict, they made popes angry. Beguine preaching would always make some men in power angry.

It didn't help that beguines tended to tolerate colorful preachers. Na Prous Boneta was inspired by Peter John Olivi, and Marguerite Porete associated with the apocalyptic preacher Guiard of Cressonessart, who announced that he had been given the title "Angel of Philadelphia" and was preparing for the immanent return of Christ. Certain Beguines did get caught up in bigger political battles, as when the church was pursuing various heretical movements.

Beguines forever had to walk a careful line between leading their unregulated and independent ways of life and ministry and not provoking the church authorities. The threat of imprisonment or death for alleged heresy was always looming. Because certain bishops, theologians, and priests would at any given time attempt to control beguines and their property, these women had to choose carefully when and where to speak out—and when to remain silent. They also needed to develop trust with town and city aldermen and mayors, with powerful theologians, and sometimes even with bishops, in order to survive. And when individual beguines were accused of heresy and did not choose a path of public defiance, they frequently moved in with monastic communities to hide from clergy and Inquisition.

While churchmen, their councils and inquisitions investigated the beguines and prosecuted some of them, in the end the religious authorities were not successful in suppressing the spirit and work of these independent medieval women and their communities.

CONCLUSION

ESPITE MANY ATTEMPTS at suppressing, even squashing, the beguines, these women and their communities survived century after century and found renewed ways to thrive. Beguines lived through many investigations conducted by the Inquisition, suffered persecution and condemnation, and survived wars, the plague, and much else. Although the Council of Vienne condemned the beguines' way of life and their numbers subsequently declined, there is a good amount of evidence—much of it only recovered in recent decades—that shows the continued presence and ministry of beguines from late medieval times all the way into the twentieth century.

Many beguine communities died out, lasting only for one or two generations. Frequently, beguine communities morphed into new expressions of the vita apostolica. As we have seen, a number of beguines aligned themselves with the Dominicans, and church authorities mostly left these "Dominican beguines" alone. Other beguines associated with the Franciscans, eventually becoming Third Order Franciscans. And certain beguines in the Low Countries joined the spiritual renewal movement *Devotio Moderna* and became known as Sisters of the Common Life. Begun by the Dutch preacher Geert Grote (1340–1384), this movement flourished in the fourteenth and fifteenth centuries. Their communities were more structured than court beguinages but less structured than monasteries. Like the beguines, these sisters created, copied, and owned various books, and the production of books was a major source of income for them.

Many smaller beguine communities in the Low Countries disappeared after around 1350, and there would have been various reasons, such as a lack of young beguines to whom ownership of a beguinage could be transferred, or a change in inheritance laws that made the transfer of home ownership from one beguine to another difficult; guilds and other competitors might have driven beguines away from a town, or the number of truly poor beguines in a beguinage might have overwhelmed its finances. But the larger court beguinages survived, often for hundreds of years. In various parts of Europe, beguine life continued and even expanded, with women forming new communities. For example, Strasbourg in 1400 had a great number of women's religious houses: eighty-five beguinages alongside seven Dominican houses, two communities of Poor Clares, and a house of penitents. In 1427 in the region of Florence, fifty-nine women were recorded living as pinzochere. In a document from 1451 in Cologne, ninety-one beguine houses were listed.

Any number of new living arrangements was possible. For instance, in 1477 Duchess Marie of Burgundy transferred the buildings of the court beguinage of Champfleury to a local Cistercian community of women whose own monastery had been destroyed in wartime. But the beguines refused to leave their home. Both groups of women brought their case to Archduke Maximilian of Austria, and they were ordered to coexist in the same complex, with the Cistercian nuns given control of the chapel, but both groups were to use it.

Another example is the beguinage *Convent van Betlehem*, which was founded in 1440 in Oisterwijk (east of Tilburg). Maria van Hout (c. 1470–1547) served as magistra there as of 1530. In 1545, at the request of the Carthusians Gerard Kalckbrenner and Johannes Lansperger of Cologne (who were impressed by her mystical writings), Maria moved with several other beguines to the Carthusian monastery of St. Barbara near Cologne. There Kalckbrenner, who considered Maria his spiritual advisor, edited and published her letters and treatises. She had crafted a series of devotional exercises centered on meditations on the wounds of Christ that the Carthusians wanted to disseminate among spiritual seekers. The Jesuit theologian Peter Canisius also visited and consulted with Maria, and Lansperger integrated some of her writings into his own published work of theology.

During the Dutch Revolt of 1565–66 (the first of a series of revolts by the Dutch against Spanish rule), local beguine communities there were plundered and severely damaged or destroyed. Yet women soon joined the surviving beguines and another round of construction of beguinages began. In 1578, the Great Beguinage in Mechelen was destroyed. Beguines returned and their new chapel was consecrated in 1596. Also in 1578, a group of beguines in Amsterdam were able to continue their beguine lifestyle by becoming caretakers of orphaned girls. And around 1612, after repairs from war damage were completed, St. Elizabeth in Kortrijk began enlarging its complex.

The Protestant Reformation and Catholic Counterreformation swept across Europe in the sixteenth century, and beguines, like all the people, were impacted by growing religious and political divisions. It was up to each local ruler to decide whether his land would become Protestant or remain Catholic, and all his subordinates were expected to follow suit. Some newly formed Protestant regimes required their local nuns—and, by association, their local beguines—to marry, whether the women wanted to or not. But historical records indicate that beguine communities decided for themselves whether to join the Protestant movement or to remain Catholic, despite their local ruler's decision. Contrary to secular authorities, some beguine communities decided to allow each member to choose which Sunday service—Catholic or Protestant—to attend, in addition to their common life of prayer and ministry. Some beguine communities endured "house arrest" when they refused to become Protestant or marry. There were beguinages that embraced the Reformation while remaining friends with Catholic beguines. They all shared common interests in ministry and a common beguine spirituality.

For example, around 1533 the region of Münster had been taken over by a Protestant reform movement called the Anabaptists.[1] Attempting to set up "God's Kingdom on earth," they called themselves the Anabaptist Kingdom of Münster. They encouraged the practice of polygamy and thus beguines were ordered to marry. Some beguines fled Münster, while others lived under house arrest in their own homes for refusing to cooperate. But the Anabaptist Kingdom soon disintegrated, and the beguines were able to resume their regular life.

In 1571, visitations were conducted by Catholic authorities at many of the beguinages in Münster, and the subsequent report indicated that the beguines were vibrant and confident—the women knew their Psalter by heart, read excellent spiritual books, and their confessor was a Catholic priest. The magistra led by example and shared authority with fellow beguines. On Sundays and feast days, "the Gospel and the Epistle were read at the table with expositions of the Church Fathers."[2] These beguines remained on good terms with their Protestant neighbors.

Town documents of Münster and the records of an ecclesiastical visitation there in 1683 reveal that women were still living as beguines, despite efforts to force them into strict enclosure or into an established order. And records a few years later state that beguines were economically active and recognized by legal authorities as beguines. Beguinages in the region of Münster were effectively suppressed only in 1809.

The Catholic Church in the 1500s, recognizing its need for reform, convened the Council of Trent (1545–63). Among the Council's many decrees was one insisting that *all* religious women profess solemn vows under strict enclosure, including religious laywomen such as beguines and penitentiae. Furthermore, the Council attempted to deny beguines any legitimacy.

Yet many beguines and like-minded laywomen continued their commitment to active ministry, seeking secular legal protection from the church. For example, in seventeenth-century France, laywomen wanted to minister among those suffering from poverty, disease, and illiteracy. The women gathered in their favorite chapels for prayer and formed associations or confraternities in order to minister more effectively. As beguines had been doing for several hundred years, these French women protected themselves legally from church interference by registering their associations as secular corporations (and not as religious gatherings) with the government.

These French charitable companies of women, successful in outmaneuvering church authorities, took on names that reflected their personal devotion or the name of their chapel. Two of the first organizations to emerge were the *Filles de Saint-Joseph du Puy*

(Daughters of St. Joseph) around 1649 and the *Filles de la Charité* (Daughters of Charity), founded by Louise de Marillac (1591–1660). Eventually, many of these informal gatherings of women in ministry morphed into formal religious communities of women.

What church authorities failed to accomplish—eradicating an informal movement of independent women—secularization in the 1800s did (for the most part) accomplish. Far more damaging to the beguines than the era of religious wars in the sixteenth and seventeenth centuries was the French Revolution and the secularization under Napoleon that swept across Europe in the subsequent decades.

With the advent of the French Revolution, many forms of religious life were nearly destroyed. Monasteries were sacked and nuns and monks were either killed or driven away. Churches were destroyed or were converted to nonreligious uses. Secular governments took possession not only of monasteries but also of beguinages and sold the women's homes to new owners. Many beguines now disappeared from historical records.

In Belgium, for example, prior to the French Revolution some forty beguine convents and court beguinages still operated, with over five hundred women living in the *Groot Beguinage* of Brussels alone. Even during the secularization, many beguine communities tried to regain title to their homes but failed. In 1825 there were twenty-six surviving beguinages in Belgium, with about 1,800 beguines living in them. Beguinages in northern France had all but disappeared by 1855, but seventeen beguinages in the southern Low Countries survived into the twentieth century (in 1900 there were still 1,230 known beguines there). Some beguinages had also survived in northern Holland and in the northern German cities of Bremen and Hamburg.

———

Even if the very last "traditional" beguine died in 2013, these women, over many centuries, have left us a great legacy: the court beguinages that are still standing as well as superb mystical literature, artwork, illuminated books, and significant contributions to theology. The beguines also left us a more hidden legacy of healing ministry and passionate preaching. But possibly the most important legacy of the beguines is their bold vision for the possibilities of community: intentional communities committed to working for and with the marginalized and carried by a love for beauty and creation.

Beguines showed great strength and persistence and collaborated with fellow seekers, tolerated diversity, and raised difficult questions; they exercised both communal and personal wisdom and freedom to follow God as they felt called. The story of the beguines affirms that women have contributed far more to spirituality and culture than history books have traditionally acknowledged. Their voices proclaim a divine presence that yearns for relationship with each of us. These medieval women offer us hope and a fresh path: to think creatively, to collaborate to achieve change, and to live with prophetic courage.

ACKNOWLEDGMENTS

Selections from *Agnes Blannbekin, Viennese Beguine: Life and Revelations*, translated with introduction by Ulrike Wiethaus, copyright Boydell & Brewer, Rochester, NY, are reprinted by permission of Boydell & Brewer, www.boydellandbrewer.com

Selections from *Angela of Foligno: Complete Works*, translated with an Introduction by Paul Lachance, O.F.M. Preface by Romana Guarnieri, copyright Paulist Press, Mahwah, NJ, are reprinted by permission of Paulist Press, www.paulistpress.com

Selections from *The Book of Prayer of Sor María of Santo Domingo* by Mary E. Giles, copyright State University of New York, Albany, are reprinted by permission of State University of New York Press, www.sunypress.edu

Selections from *Beghinae in cantu instructae: Musical Patrimony from Flemish Beguinages (Middle Ages–Late 18th C.)*, edited by Pieter Mannaerts, copyright Brepols, Turnhout, Belgium, are reprinted by permission of Brepols Publishers, www.brepols.net

Selections from *Catherine of Genoa: Purgation and Purgatory, The Spiritual Dialogue*, translated and notes by Serge Hughes, copyright Paulist Press, Mahwah, NJ, are reprinted by permission of Paulist Press, www.paulistpress.com

Selections from *Hadewijch: The Complete Works*, translated by Mother Columba Hart, OSB, copyright Paulist Press, Mahwah, NJ, are reprinted by permission of Paulist Press, www.paulistpress.com

Selections from *The Life of Saint Douceline, a Beguine of Provence*, translated with introduction by Kathleen E. Garay and Madeleine Jeay, copyright Boydell & Brewer, Rochester, NY, are reprinted by permission of Boydell & Brewer, www.boydellandbrewer.com

Selections from *A Little Daily Wisdom*, edited by Carmen Acevedo Butcher, copyright Paraclete Press, Orleans, MA, are reprinted by permission of Paraclete Press, www.paracletepress.com

Selections from *Marguerite Porete: The Mirror of Simple Souls*, translated and introduced by Ellen L. Babinsky, copyright Paulist Press, Mahwah, NJ, are reprinted by permission of Paulist Press, www.paulistpress.com

Selections from *Mary of Oignies: Mother of Salvation*, edited by Anneke B. Mulder-Bakker, copyright Brepols, Turnhout, Belgium, are reprinted by permission of Brepols Publishers, www.brepols.net

Selections from *Medieval Holy Women in the Christian Tradition c. 1100–c. 1500*, edited by Alastair Minnis and Rosalynn Voaden, copyright Brepols, Turnhout, Belgium, are reprinted by permission of Brepols Publishers, www.brepols.net

Selections from *Medieval Women's Visionary Literature*, edited by Elizabeth Alvilda Petroff, copyright Oxford University Press, New York, are reprinted by permission of Oxford University Press, www.oup.org

NOTES

1. WHO WERE THE BEGUINES?

1. The debate about the origins of the nickname "beguine" has been settled to my satisfaction by Walter Simons (see Walter Simons in *Beghinae in cantu instructae*, p. 16).
2. This was considered an acceptable form of informal divorce in medieval times.
3. Galatians 3:28.

2. BEGUINES ACROSS EUROPE

1. See *Mary of Oignies*, p. 125. I rely on Mulder-Bakker's research for this section.
2. *Mary of Oignies*, p. 48.
3. See Simons, *Cities of Ladies*, appendix I.
4. See Simons, *Cities of Ladies*, pp. 256ff. I rely on Simons's research for the founding statistics in this section.
5. See Simons, *Cities of Ladies*, p. 54. I rely on Simons's research for this section.
6. *The Life of Saint Douceline, a Beguine of Provence*, p. 34.
7. See, for example, Mazzonis, *Spirituality, Gender, and the Self in Renaissance Italy*, p. 2.
8. *Agnes Blannbekin, Viennese Beguine*, p. 103.
9. In this section, I rely on *Medieval Holy Women in the Christian Tradition c. 1100– c. 1500* (in particular the research of Ronald E. Surz, pp. 503ff), and on Perry, *Gender and Disorder in Early Modern Seville*.
10. See Perry, *Gender and Disorder in Early Modern Seville*, p. 97.
11. "Confessor" in medieval Europe was comparable to our present-day use of Spiritual Director or Spiritual Companion.
12. See Bilinkoff, *The Ávila of Saint Teresa*, pp. 39ff.

3. THE BEGUINAGE

1. Historic records show that a number of court beguinages that had sprung up around an infirmary had chosen to keep the legal foundation documents in the name of the infirmary, a practice that reveals how important the ministry to the vulnerable was to the beguines.
2. See Simons, *Cities of Ladies*, p. 55 and p. 181, note 103. This phrase was first used in 1288 by Jan Broeckaert regarding Dendermonde.
3. See Simons, *Cities of Ladies*, p. 55.
4. See Simons, *Cities of Ladies*, p. 267 (25A).
5. Panzer, *Cistercian Women and the Beguines*, p. 141.
6. See Simons, *Cities of Ladies*, pp. 72–73.
7. See Simons, *Cities of Ladies*, p. 73.
8. "The Brabant Mystic: Hadewijch," in *Medieval Women Writers*, p. 197.

4. BEGUINE MINISTRIES

1. Simons, *Cities of Ladies*, p. 76.
2. See Penelope Galloway in *New Trends in Feminine Spirituality*, p. 113. Ghillain de Saint Venant's son executed her will in January 1261.
3. See Penelope Galloway in *New Trends in Feminine Spirituality*, p. 112.
4. See Simons, *Cities of Ladies*, p. 106.
5. See Gelser, *Lay Religious Women and Church Reform in Late Medieval Munster*, p. 171.
6. See Gill, *Penitents, Pinzochere and Mantellate*, p. 240.

7. Ledòchowska, *Angela Merici and the Company of St. Ursula*, p. 67.
8. See Simons, *Cities of Ladies*, p. 81.
9. See Simons, *Cities of Ladies*, p. 97. Simons dates the letter to 1284. "Holy Ghost" and "Holy Spirit" are interchangeable terms.
10. *A Little Daily Wisdom*, pp. 146–47.

5. BEGUINE SPIRITUALITY

1. I have taken literary license by using some of the words of Angela of Foligno for this fictional magistra; I have adapted these words from Angela of Foligno's *Instructions*, as in *A Little Daily Wisdom*, p. 168.
2. See Warren, *The Embodied Word*, and McNamer, *Affective Meditation and the Invention of Medieval Compassion*.
3. *The Life of Saint Douceline, a Beguine of Provence*, p. 33.
4. Several of these liturgical cradles survive: for example, in the Grand Beguinage in Leuven and in The Metropolitan Museum of Art, New York.
5. *Life of Blessed Juliana of Mont-Cornillon*, p. 44.
6. *The Life of Saint Douceline, a Beguine of Provence*, pp. 59–60.
7. *Thomas of Cantimpré: The Collected Saints' Lives*, pp. 172–73. Visions that reported a conversation between a beguine and Mary or Jesus or a saint were not uncommon.
8. *Medieval Holy Women in the Christian Tradition c. 1100–c. 1500*, p. 588.
9. See *Angela of Foligno*. I rely on Angela of Foligno's *Instructions* (XXVIII) for this section.
10. See Bynum, "Women Mystics and Eucharistic Devotion in the Thirteenth Century."
11. *Medieval Women's Visionary Literature*, p. 192. The quote is from Hadewijch's sixth letter to a young beguine.
12. *Agnes Blannbekin, Viennese Beguine*, p. 119.
13. *Hadewijch*, p. 280.
14. *Life of Blessed Juliana of Mont-Cornillon*, p. 47.
15. *Hadewijch*, p. 281.
16. Bynum, "Women Mystics and Eucharistic Devotion in the Thirteenth Century," p. 179.
17. *Thomas of Cantimpré: The Collected Saints' Lives*, p. 165.
18. See Bynum, "Women Mystics and Eucharistic Devotion in the Thirteenth Century," p. 193.
19. *A Little Daily Wisdom*, p. 94.
20. *Agnes Blannbekin, Viennese Beguine*, p. 146.

6. BEGUINE COMPASSION

1. See Le Goff, *The Birth of Purgatory*, p. 39.
2. Newman, *From Virile Woman to WomanChrist*, p. 109. Newman notes (on p. 111) that Hildegard of Bingen wrote a work called *Liber vitae meritorum* (*Book of Life's Merits*) that was devoted to purgatory.
3. Le Goff suggests that "purgatory" had been an adjective until the late twelfth century, when it became a noun.
4. *Mary of Oignies*, pp. 63–64.
5. See Barbara Newman's Introduction in *Thomas of Cantimpré: The Collected Saints' Lives*.
6. I rely here on *Thomas of Cantimpré: The Collected Saints' Lives*.
7. See *Thomas of Cantimpré: The Collected Saints' Lives*, p. 257.
8. See *Thomas of Cantimpré: The Collected Saints' Lives*, pp. 293–94.

9. See Newman, *From Virile Woman to WomanChrist*, p. 112.

10. See Le Goff, *The Birth of Purgatory*, pp. 319–20.

11. Mechthild of Magdeburg, *The Flowing Light of the Godhead*, Book VII, p. 21.

12. Le Goff, *The Birth of Purgatory*, pp. 331–32.

13. See Newman, *From Virile Woman to WomanChrist*, chapter 4.

14. *Catherine of Genoa*, p. 71. The quote is from *Purgation and Purgatory*.

15. *A Little Daily Wisdom*, pp. 97–98.

16. *Agnes Blannbekin, Viennese Beguine*, p. 99.

17. *Thomas of Cantimpré: The Collected Saints' Lives*, p. 140.

18. See Benedict Groeschel's Introduction in *Catherine of Genoa*, especially p. 35.

19. Chervin, *Prayers of the Women Mystics*, pp. 105–6.

7. BEGUINES AS PREACHERS AND PERFORMERS

1. See *Thomas of Cantimpré: The Collected Saints' Lives*, pp. 127–28.

2. *Thomas of Cantimpré: The Collected Saints' Lives*, p. 151.

3. *Thomas of Cantimpré: The Collected Saints' Lives*, pp. 145–46.

4. See Ross, *The Grief of God*, p. 110.

5. *Vita Elizabeth sanctimonialis in Erkenrode*, private translation graciously provided by Jesse Njus (section 3).

6. *Vita Elizabeth sanctimonialis in Erkenrode*, private translation graciously provided by Jesse Njus (section 6).

7. Abbot Philip was quite detailed in what he witnessed and examined, stating: "Therefore, it must be known that the aforementioned girl most plainly carries on her body the stigmata of our Lord Jesus Christ; she carries them on her hands and feet and side, without any suspicion of pretense or the slightest bit of fraud, for the fresh wounds are most clearly visible and frequently discharge a stream of blood on Fridays. The wounds in her hands and feet are round while that in her side is oblong, as if the former indicate the pressing of nails, the latter of a spear . . ." The quote is from *Vita Elizabeth sanctimonialis in Erkenrode*, private translation graciously provided by Jesse Njus (section 3).

8. *Vita Elizabeth sanctimonialis in Erkenrode*, private translation graciously provided by Jesse Njus (section 30).

9. *Vita Elizabeth sanctimonialis in Erkenrode*, private translation graciously provided by Jesse Njus (section 27).

10. *Medieval Women's Visionary Literature*, p. 214.

11. See *Marguerite Porete*.

12. See *Agnes Blannbekin, Viennese Beguine*, chapters 214 and 215.

13. Suydam, "Writing Beguines," p. 141.

14. See Suzanne Noffke in *Medieval Holy Women in the Christian Tradition c. 1100– c. 1500*, pp. 603–5.

15. *A Little Daily Wisdom*, p. 242.

16. See Suzanne Noffke in *Medieval Holy Women in the Christian Tradition c. 1100– c. 1500*, p. 613.

17. *A Little Daily Wisdom*, p. 16.

18. In this section, I rely on Giles, *The Book of Prayer of Sor María of Santo Domingo*.

19. Giles, *The Book of Prayer of Sor María of Santo Domingo*, p. 169.

20. Giles, *The Book of Prayer of Sor María of Santo Domingo*, pp. 172–73.

8. LITERARY BEGUINES

1. See *The Voice of Silence*, pp. 116–17.

2. See Simons, "Staining the Speech of Things Divine," p. 106.

3. Mechthild of Magdeburg, *The Flowing Light of the Godhead*, p. 39.
4. See Ulrike Wiethaus in *Christian Spirituality*, p. 103.
5. See Amy Hollywood and Patricia Z. Beckman in *Medieval Holy Women in the Christian Tradition c. 1100–c. 1500*, p. 418.
6. *Medieval Women's Visionary Literature*, p. 214.
7. *A Little Daily Wisdom*, p. 139.
8. *Medieval Women Writers*, p. 170.
9. Mechthild of Magdeburg, *The Flowing Light of the Godhead*, p. 250.
10. Mechthild von Magdeburg, *Flowing Light of the Divinity*, pp. 56–57.
11. *Medieval Women Writers*, pp. 170–71.
12. For this section, I rely on Straeten, "A Study of Beatrice of Nazareth's *Van seuen manieren van heiliger minnen–Of seven manners of holy loving*," and Eric Colledge in *Medieval Women's Visionary Literature*. See also Else Marie Wiberg Pedersen in *New Trends in Feminine Spirituality*, pp. 61ff.
13. *Medieval Women's Visionary Literature*, p. 200.
14. Straeten, "A Study of Beatrice of Nazareth's *Van seuen manieren van heiliger minnen–Of seven manners of holy loving*," p. 12.
15. Straeten, "A Study of Beatrice of Nazareth's *Van seuen manieren van heiliger minnen–Of seven manners of holy loving*," p. 13.
16. Straeten, "A Study of Beatrice of Nazareth's *Van seuen manieren van heiliger minnen–Of seven manners of holy loving*," p. 15.
17. See Straeten, "A Study of Beatrice of Nazareth's *Van seuen manieren van heiliger minnen–Of seven manners of holy loving*," p. 14.
18. See Ria Vanderauwera in *Medieval Women Writers*, p. 189.
19. *Hadewijch*, p. 86. The quote is from Hadewijch's Letter 18.
20. Baumer-Despeigne, "Hadewijch of Antwerp and Hadewijch II," p. 26. The quote is from Hadewijch's Letter 6.
21. *A Little Daily Wisdom*, p. 177.

9. WERE BEGUINES HERETICS?
1. I am indebted to John Van Engen for this insight.
2. *A Mirror for Simple Souls*, p. 23.
3. *Marguerite Porete*, p. 33.
4. Southern, *Western Society and the Church in the Middle Ages*, p. 329.
5. Bolton, "Some Thirteenth-Century Women in the Low Countries," p. 20.
6. See Simons, *Cities of Ladies*, p. 114.
7. *The Voice of Silence*, p. 90.
8. See Gill, *Penitents, Pinzochere and Mantellate*, p. 144, note 1.
9. Burnham, *So Great a Light, So Great a Smoke*, p. 147.
10. *Medieval Women's Visionary Literature*, p. 290.
11. See Ahlgren, *Teresa of Avila and the Politics of Sanctity*, pp. 23ff.
12. See Mary E. Giles in *Women in the Inquisition*, p. 77.
13. *Francisca de los Apóstoles: The Inquisition of Francisca*, p. 53.
14. See Perry, *Gender and Disorder in Early Modern Seville*, pp. 105ff.

CONCLUSION
1. I rely on Gelser, *Lay Religious Women and Church Reform in Late Medieval Munster* for this section.
2. Gelser, *Lay Religious Women and Church Reform in Late Medieval Munster*, p. 337.

BIBLIOGRAPHY

Many publications on the beguines are in Dutch, German, or French. Here I am including only select works in English. Many of these studies include excellent bibliographies of both other studies in English as well as studies in other languages.

Agnes Blannbekin, Viennese Beguine: Life and Revelations, translated with introduction by Ulrike Wiethaus. Cambridge, UK/Rochester, NY: D. S. Brewer, 2002.

Ahlgren, Gillian T.W., "Teresa of Avila and Angela of Foligno: Ecstatic Sisters." *Magistra: A Journal of Women's Spirituality in History* 11:1 (Summer 2005): 83–105.

_____, *Teresa of Avila and the Politics of Sanctity*. Ithaca, NY: Cornell University Press, 1996.

Angela of Foligno: Complete Works, translated with an Introduction by Paul Lachance, O.F.M. Preface by Romana Guarnieri. New York/Mahwah, NJ: Paulist Press, 1993.

Babinsky, Ellen L., *A Beguine in the Court of the King: The Relation of Love and Knowledge in the Mirror of Simple Souls by Marguerite Porete*. Ph.D., University of Chicago, 1991.

Bartoli, Marco, *Saint Clare: Beyond the Legend*, translated by Sister Frances Teresa Downing. Cincinnati, OH: St. Anthony Messenger Press, 2010.

Baumer-Despeigne, Odette, "Hadewijch of Antwerp and Hadewijch II: Mysticism of Being in the Thirteenth Century in Brabant." *Studia Mystica* (Winter 1991): 16–38.

Beghinae in cantu instructae: Musical Patrimony from Flemish Beguinages (Middle Ages–Late 18th Century), edited by Pieter Mannaerts. Turnhout, Belgium: Brepols, 2009.

Bennett, Judith M., *Sisters and Workers in the Middle Ages*. Chicago: University of Chicago Press, 1989.

Bilinkoff, Jodi, *The Ávila of Saint Teresa: Religious Reform in a Sixteenth-Century City*. Ithaca, NY: Cornell University Press, 1989.

Bollmann, Anne, "'Being a Woman on my Own': Alijt Bake (1415–1455) as Reformer of the Inner Self." In *Seeing and Knowing: Women and Learning in Medieval Europe 1200–1550*, edited by Anneke B. Mulder-Bakker, 67–96. Turnhout, Belgium: Brepols, 2004.

Bolton, Brenda M., "Mulieres Sanctae." In *Sanctity and Secularity: The Church and the World* (Studies in Church History 10), edited by Derek Baker, 77–95. Oxford: Blackwell, 1973.

_____, "Some Thirteenth-Century Women in the Low Countries: A Special Case?" *Nederlands Archief voor Kerkgeschiedenis* 61:1 (1981): 7–29.

_____, "*Vitae Matrum*: A Further Aspect of the *Frauenfrage*." In *Medieval Women: Studies in Church History*, edited by Derek Baker, 253–74. Oxford: Basil Blackwell, 1978.

Bowie, Fiona, and Oliver Davies, *Beguine Spirituality: Mystical Writings of Mechthild of Magdeburg, Beatrice of Nazareth, and Hadewijch of Brabant*. New York: Crossroad, 1990.

Brasher, Sally, "Toward a Revised View of Medieval Women and the *Vita Apostolica*: The Humiliati and the Beguines Compared." *Magistra: A Journal of Women's Spirituality in History* 11:2 (Winter 2005): 1–33.

_____, *Women of the Humiliati: A Lay Religious Order in Medieval Civic Life*. New York: Routledge, 2003.

Brophy, Don, *Catherine of Siena: A Passionate Life*. New York: BlueBridge, 2010.

Brown, Jennifer, "Elizabeth of Spalbeek's Body: *Performatio Christi*." *Magistra: A Journal of Women's Spirituality in History* 11:2 (Winter 2005): 70–88.

_____, *Three Women of Liege: A Critical Edition of and Commentary on the Middle English Lives of Elizabeth of Spalbeek, Christina Mirabilis, and Marie d'Oignies*. Turnhout, Belgium: Brepols, 2008.

Brown, Melissa, "Marie d'Oignies, Marguerite Porete and 'Authentic' Female Mystic Piety in the Middle Ages." In *Worshipping Women: Misogyny and Mysticism in the Middle Ages*, edited by John O. Ward and Francesca C. Bussey, 187–235. Sydney: University of Sydney Press, 1997.

Burnham, Louisa A., *So Great a Light, So Great a Smoke: The Beguin Heretics of Languedoc*. Ithaca, NY: Cornell University Press, 2008.

Bynum, Caroline Walker, *Fragmentation and Redemption: Essays on Gender and the Human Body in Medieval Religion*. New York: Zone, 1991.

_____, *Holy Feast and Holy Fast: The Religious Significance of Food to Medieval Women*. Berkeley: University of California Press, 1987.

_____, *Jesus as Mother: Studies in the Spirituality of the High Middle Ages*. Berkeley: University of California Press, 1982.

_____, "Women Mystics and Eucharistic Devotion in the Thirteenth Century." *Women's Studies* 11 (1984): 179–214.

Cant, Geneviève de, *A World of Independent Women from the 12th Century to the Present Day: The Flemish Beguinages*. Riverside, CT: Herve van Caloen Foundation, 2003.

Carpenter, Jennifer, "Juette of Huy, Recluse and Mother (1158–1228): Children and Mothering in the Saintly Life." In *Power of the Weak: Studies on Medieval Women*, edited by Jennifer Carpenter and Sally-Beth MacLean, 57–93. Urbana and Chicago: University of Illinois Press, 1995.

Catherine of Genoa: Purgation and Purgatory, The Spiritual Dialogue, translated and notes by Serge Hughes. New York/Mahwah, NJ: Paulist Press, 1979.

Catherine of Siena: The Dialogue, translated and with an Introduction by Suzanne Noffke, O.P. New York/Mahwah, NJ: Paulist Press, 1980.

Chatellier, Louis, *The Europe of the Devout: The Catholic Reformation and the Formation of a New Society*, translated by Jean Birrell. Cambridge, UK: Cambridge University Press, 1989.

Chervin, Ronda de Sola, *Prayers of the Women Mystics*. Ann Arbor, MI: Servant Publications, 1992.

Cho, Min-Ah, "Deadly Loneliness, Deadly Bliss: Rethinking Spirituality in Light of Hadewijch of Antwerp's Writing About Union with Love." *Magistra: A Journal of Women's Spirituality in History* 15:2 (Winter 2009): 3–19.

Christensen, Kristen Marie, "In the Beguine Was the Word: Mysticism and Catholic Reformation in the Devotional Literature of Maria van Hout (+1547)." In *Seeing and Knowing: Women and Learning in Medieval Europe 1200–1550*, edited by Anneke B. Mulder-Bakker, 97–120. Turnhout, Belgium: Brepols, 2004.

Christianity in Western Europe, c. 1100 –c. 1500, edited by Miri Rubin and Walter Simons. Cambridge, UK: Cambridge University Press, 2009.

Christian Spirituality: The Classics, edited by Arthur Holder. New York: Routledge, 2009.

Coakley, John, "Friars as Confidants of Holy Women in Medieval Dominican Hagiography." In *Images of Sainthood in Medieval Europe*, edited by Renate Blumenfeld-Kosinski and Timea Szell, 222–46. Ithaca, NY: Cornell University Press, 1991.

_____, "Gender and Authority of the Friars: The Significance of Holy Women for Thirteenth-Century Franciscans and Dominicans." *Church History* 60 (1991).

_____, *Women, Men, and Spiritual Power: Female Saints and Their Male Collaborators*. New York: Columbia University Press, 2006.

Conn, Marie A., *Noble Daughters: Unheralded Women in Western Christianity, 13th to 18th Centuries*. Westport, CT: Greenwood Press.

Constable, Giles, *The Reformation of the Twelfth Century*. Cambridge, UK: Cambridge University Press, 1996.

Deane, Jennifer Kolpacoff, "'Beguines' Reconsidered: Historiographical Problems and New Directions." *Monastic Matrix*, Commentaria 3461 (August 2008).

_____, "Did Beguines Have a Late-Medieval Crisis? Historical Models and Historiographical Martyrs." *Early Modern Women* 9 (2014).

_____, *A History of Medieval Heresy and Inquisition* (Critical Issues in World and International History). Lanham, MD: Rowman & Littlefield, 2011.

_____, *Labels and Libels: Naming Beguines in Northern Medieval Europe*, edited by Jennifer Deane, Letha Böhringer, and Hildo van Engen. Turnhout, Belgium: Brepols, 2014.

De Ganck, Roger, *Beatrice of Nazareth in Her Context*. Kalamazoo, MI: Cistercian Publications, 1991.

_____, *The Life of Beatrice of Nazareth: 1200–1280*. Kalamazoo, MI: Cistercian Publications, 1991.

The Dialogue of the Seraphic Virgin, Catherine of Siena, edited and translated by Algar Thorold. London: Burns, Oates & Washbourne, 1925.

Dominican Penitent Women, edited, translated, and introduced by Maiju Lehmijoki-Gardner, with contributions by Daniel Bornstein and E. Ann Matter. New York/Mahwah, NJ: Paulist Press, 2005.

Donovan, Richard B., *The Liturgical Drama in Medieval Spain*. Toronto: Pontifical Institute of Medieval Studies, 1958.

Dreyer, Elizabeth A., *Passionate Spirituality: Hildegard of Bingen and Hadewijch of Brabant*. New York/Mahwah, NJ: Paulist Press, 2005.

Duffy, Eamon, *Marking the Hours: English People and Their Prayers, 1240–1570*. New Haven, CT: Yale University Press, 2006.

Eisen, Ute E., *Women Officeholders in Early Christianity: Epigraphical and Literary Studies*. Collegeville, MN: Liturgical Press, 2000.

Elliot, Dyan, *The Bride of Christ Goes to Hell: Metaphor and Embodiment in the Lives of Pious Women, 200–1500*. Philadelphia: University of Pennsylvania Press, 2011.

_____, *Proving Woman: Female Spirituality and Inquisitorial Culture in the Later Middle Ages*. Princeton, NJ: Princeton University Press, 2004.

The Essential Writings of Christian Mysticism, edited by Bernard McGinn. New York: Modern Library, 2006.

Farmer, Sharon, *Surviving Poverty in Medieval Paris: Gender, Ideology, and the Daily Lives of the Poor*. Ithaca, NY: Cornell University Press, 2005.

Field, Sean L., *The Beguine, the Angel, and the Inquisitor: The Trials of Marguerite Porete and Guiard of Cressonessart*. Notre Dame, IN: University of Notre Dame Press, 2012.

Francisca de los Apóstoles: The Inquisition of Francisca: A Sixteenth-Century Visionary on Trial, edited and translated by Gillian T. W. Ahlgren. Chicago: University of Chicago Press, 2005.

Galea, Kate P. Crawford, "Unhappy Choices: Factors that Contributed to the Decline and Condemnation of the Beguines." In *On Pilgrimage: The Best of Ten Years of Vox Benedictina*, edited by Margot King, 505–18. Toronto: Peregrina Press, 1994.

Galloway, Penelope, "'Discreet and Devout Maidens': Women's Involvement in Beguine Communities in Northern France, 1200–1500." In *Medieval Women in Their Communities*, edited by Diane Watt, 92–115. Toronto: University of Toronto Press, 1997.

_____, *The Origins, Development and Significance of the Beguine Communities in Douai and Lille, 1200–1500*. Ph.D., University of Oxford, 1998.

Gelser, Erica, *Lay Religious Women and Church Reform in Late Medieval Munster: A Case Study*. Ph.D., University of Pennsylvania, 2008.

Gendered Voices: Medieval Saints and Their Interpreters, edited by Catherine Mooney. Philadelphia: University of Pennsylvania Press, 1999.

Giles, Mary E., *The Book of Prayer of Sor María of Santo Domingo: A Study and Translation*. Albany: State University of New York Press, 1990.

Gill, Katherine Jane, *Penitents, Pinzochere and Mantellate: Varieties of Women's Religious Communities in Central Italy, c. 1300–1520*. Ph.D., Princeton University, 1994.

_____, "Scandala: Controversies Concerning *Clausura* and Women's Religious Communities in Late Medieval Italy." In *Christendom and Its Discontents: Exclusion, Persecution, and Rebellion, 1000–1500*, edited by Scott L. Waugh and Peter D. Diehl, 177–206. Cambridge, UK: Cambridge University Press, 1996.

Gooday, Frances, "Mechthild of Magdeburg and Hadewijch of Antwerp: A Comparison." *Ons Geestelijk Erf.* 49 (1975): 305–62.

Goodrich, Michael E., *Miracles and Wonders: The Development of the Concept of Miracle, 1150–1350*. Burlington, VT: Ashgate, 2007.

Grundmann, Herbert, *Religious Movements in the Middle Ages: The Historical Links between Heresy, the Mendicant Orders, and the Women's Religious Movement in the Twelfth and Thirteenth Century, with the Historical Foundations of German Mysticism*, translated by Steven Rowan. Notre Dame, IN: University of Notre Dame Press, 1995.

Guidera, Christine, *Loving God with His Own Love: The Beguines of the Southern Low Countries in Community*. Ph.D., University of Minnesota, 2001.

Hadewijch: The Complete Works, translated by Mother Columba Hart, OSB. New York/Mahwah, NJ: Paulist Press, 1980.

Hahn, Kathleen, "A Mystic Who Dared the Church: Mechthild of Magdeburg." *Magistra: A Journal of Women's Spirituality in History* 10:2 (Winter 2004): 24–36.

Hairline, Craig, "Actives and Contemplatives: The Female Religious of the Low Countries Before and After Trent." *Catholic Historical Review* 81 (1995): 541–67.

Halvorson, Jon Derek, *Religio and Reformation: Johannes Justus Lansperger, O. Cart. (1489/90–1539), and the Sixteenth-century Religious Question*. Ph.D., Loyola University Chicago, 2008.

Hamburger, Jeffrey F., *The Rothschild Canticles: Art and Mysticism in Flanders and the Rhineland circa 1300*. New Haven, CT: Yale University Press, 1990.

Herlihy, David, *Opera Muliebria: Women and Work in Medieval Europe*. Philadelphia: Temple University Press, 1990.

Holler, Jacqueline, *Escogidas Plantas: Nuns and Beatas in Mexico City, 1531–1601*. New York: Columbia University Press, 2005.

Hollywood, Amy, *The Soul as Virgin Wife: Mechthild of Magdeburg, Marguerite Porete, and Meister Eckhart*. Notre Dame, IN: University of Notre Dame Press, 1995.

Hull, Suzanne W., *Chaste, Silent & Obedient: English Books for Women 1475–1640*. San Marino, CA: The Huntington Library, 1982.

Ida of Louvain: Medieval Cistercian Nun, translated by Martinus Cawley. Lafayette, OR: Guadalupe Translations, 1990.

Ida the Gentle of Leau: Cistercian Nun of La Ramée, translated by Martinus Cawley. Lafayette, OR: Guadalupe Translations, 1998.

Kadel, Andrew, *Matrology: A Bibliography of Writings by Christian Women from the First to the Fifteenth Centuries*. New York: Continuum, 1995.

Karras, Ruth Mazo, "Using Women to Think With in the Medieval University." In *Seeing and Knowing: Women and Learning in Medieval Europe 1200–1550*, edited by Anneke B. Mulder-Bakker, 21–34. Turnhout, Belgium: Brepols, 2004.

Kieckhefer, Richard, *Unquiet Souls: Fourteenth-Century Saints and Their Religious Milieu*. Chicago: University of Chicago Press, 1984.

King, Margot H., "The Sacramental Witness of Christina Mirabilis: The Mystic Growth of a Fool for Christ's Sake." In *Peace Weavers: Medieval Religious Women*, Vol. 2, edited by John A. Nichols and Lillian Thomas Shank, 145–64. Kalamazoo, MI: Cistercian Publications, 1987.

Kittell, Ellen E., and Mary A. Suydam, *The Texture of Society: Medieval Women in the Southern Low Countries*. New York: Palgrave Macmillan, 2004.

_____, "Women, Audience and Public Acts in Medieval Flanders." *Journal of Women's History* 10:3 (Autumn 1998): 74–96.

Knox, Lezlie, "Audacious Nuns: Institutionalizing the Franciscan Order of Saint Clare." *Church History* 69:1 (2000): 41–62.

Kocher, Suzanne, *Allegories of Love in Marguerite Porete's* Mirror of Simple Souls. Turnhout, Belgium: Brepols, 2009.

Koorn, Florence, "Women without Vows: The Case of the Beguines and the Sisters of the Common Life in the Northern Netherlands." In *Women and Men in Spiritual Culture, XIV–XVII Centuries: A Meeting of South and North*, edited by Paul E. Szarmach. Albany: State University of New York Press, 1984.

Ledòchowska, Teresa, *Angela Merici and the Company of St. Ursula*. Rome and Milan: Ancora Press, 1968.

Le Goff, Jacques, *The Birth of Purgatory*, translated by Arthur Goldhammer. Chicago: University of Chicago Press, 1983.

Lichtmann, Maria, "Marguerite Porete." In *Christian Spirituality: The Classics*, edited by Arthur Holder. New York: Routledge, 2009.

The Life of Blessed Juliana of Mont-Cornillon, translated by Barbara Newman. Toronto: Peregrina, 1988.

The Life of Christina the Astonishing, by Thomas de Cantimpré, translated by Margot H. King. Toronto: Peregrina, 1989.

The Life of Margaret of Ypres, by Thomas de Cantimpré, translated by Margot H. King. Toronto: Peregrina, 1990.

The Life of Saint Douceline, a Beguine of Provence, translated with introduction by Kathleen E. Garay and Madeleine Jeay. Woodbridge, UK: D. S. Brewer, 2001.

A Little Daily Wisdom, edited by Carmen Acevedo Butcher. Brewster, MA: Paraclete Press, 2005.

Lives of Ida of Nivelles, Lutgard and Alice the Leper, translated by Martinus Cawley. Lafayette, OR: Guadalupe Translations, 1987.

Living Saints of the Thirteenth Century: The Lives of Yvette, Anchoress of Huy; Juliana of Cornillon, Inventor of the Corpus Christi Feast; Margaret the Lame, Anchoress of Magdeburg, edited by Anneke B. Mulder-Bakker. Turnhout, Belgium: Brepols, 2011.

Long, Mary Elizabeth, *Reading Female Sanctity: English Legendaries of Women, ca. 1200–1650*. Ph.D., University of Massachusetts, Amherst, 2004.

Luongo, F. Thomas, *The Saintly Politics of Catherine of Siena*. Ithaca, NY: Cornell University Press, 2005.

Macy, Gary, *The Banquet's Wisdom: A Short History of the Theologies of the Lord's Supper*. New York/Mahwah, NJ: Paulist Press, 1992.

Makowski, Elizabeth, *Canon Law and Cloistered Women: Periculoso and Its Commentators 1298–1545*. Washington, DC: Catholic University of America Press, 1997.

_____, "*Mulieres Religiosae*, Strictly Speaking: Some Fourteenth-Century Canonical Opinions." *Catholic Historical Review* 85 (1999): 1–14.

Marguerite Porete: The Mirror of Simple Souls, translated and introduced by Ellen L. Babinsky. New York/Mahwah, NJ: Paulist Press, 1993.

Mary of Oignies: Mother of Salvation, edited by Anneke B. Mulder-Bakker, translations by Margot H. King and Hugh Feiss, and with contributions by Brenda Bolton and Suzan Folkerts. Turnhout, Belgium: Brepols, 2006.

Mazzonis, Querciolo, *Spirituality, Gender, and the Self in Renaissance Italy: Angela Merici and the Company of St. Ursula (1474–1540)*. Washington, DC: Catholic University of America Press, 2007.

McDonnell, Ernest William, *The Beguines and Beghards in Medieval Culture, with Special Emphasis on the Belgian Scene*. New York: Octagon Books, 1969.

McGinn, Bernard, *The Flowering of Mysticism: Men and Women in the New Mysticism, 1200–1350*. New York: Crossroad, 1998.

_____, *Meister Eckhart and the Beguine Mystics*. New York: Continuum, 1994.

McKelvie, Roberta A., *Retrieving a Living Tradition: Angelina of Montegiove, Franciscan, Tertiary, Beguine*. St. Bonaventure, NY: Franciscan Institute, St. Bonaventure University, 1997.

McNamara, Jo Ann, *Sisters in Arms: Nuns through Two Millennia*. Cambridge, MA: Harvard University Press, 1996.

McNamer, Sarah, *Affective Meditation and the Invention of Medieval Compassion*. Philadelphia: University of Pennsylvania Press, 2010.

Mechthild of Magdeburg, *The Flowing Light of the Godhead*, translated by Frank Tobin. New York/Mahwah, NJ: Paulist Press, 1998.

Mechthild von Magdeburg, *Flowing Light of the Divinity*, translated by Christiane Mesch Galvani, edited by Susan Clark. New York: Garland Publishing, 1991.

Medieval Holy Women in the Christian Tradition c. 1100–c. 1500, edited by Alastair Minnis and Rosalynn Voaden. Turnhout, Belgium: Brepols, 2010.

Medieval Women's Visionary Literature, edited by Elizabeth Alvilda Petroff. New York: Oxford University Press, 1986.

Medieval Women Writers, edited by Katharina M. Wilson. Athens, GA: University of Georgia Press, 1984.

Milhaven, John Giles, *Hadewijch and Her Sisters: Other Ways of Loving and Knowing*. Albany: State University of New York Press, 1993.

Miller, Tanya Stabler, *The Beguines of Medieval Paris: Gender, Patronage, and Spiritual Authority*. Philadelphia: University of Pennsylvania Press, 2014.

_____, "'Love is Beguine': Labeling Lay Religiosity in Thirteenth-Century Paris." In *Labels, Libels, and Lay Religious Women in Northern Medieval Europe*, edited by Jennifer Kolpakoff Deane, Hildo von Engen, and Letha Boehringer. Turnhout, Belgium: Brepols, 2014.

_____, "Mirror of the Scholarly (Masculine) Soul: Thinking with Beguines in the Colleges of Medieval Paris." In *Negotiating Clerical Identities: Priests, Monks and Masculinity in the Middle Ages*, edited by Jennifer D. Thibodeaux, 238–64. New York: Palgrave Macmillan, 2010.

_____, *Now She Is Martha, Now She Is Mary: Beguine Communities in Medieval Paris (1250–1470)*. Ph.D., University of California at Santa Barbara, 2007.

_____, "What's in a Name? Clerical Representation of Parisian Beguines (1200–1328)." *Journal of Medieval History* 33:1 (2007): 60–86.

A Mirror for Simple Souls: The Mystical Work of Marguerite Porete, edited and translated by Charles Crawford. New York: Crossroad, 1990.

Mommaers, Paul, with Elisabeth Dutton, *Hadewijch: Writer–Beguine–Love Mystic*. Leuven: Peeters, 2004.

More, Alison, *In Hortiis Liliorum Domini: A Study of Feminine Piety in Medieval Flanders with Particular Reference to the Vitae of the Mulieres Sanctae*. Ph.D., Queen's University, 2000.

Morrison, Molly, "Christ's Body in the Visions of Angela of Foligno." *Magistra: A Journal of Women's Spirituality in History* 10:2 (Winter 2004): 37–59.

Mother Mary Francis, *The Testament of St. Colette*. Chicago: Franciscan Herald Press, 1987.

Muessig, Carolyn, "Performance of the Passion: The Enactment of Devotion in the Later Middle Ages." In *Visualizing Medieval Performance: Perspectives, Histories, Contexts*, edited by Elina Gertsman, 129–42. Burlington, VT: Ashgate, 2008.

Mulder-Bakker, Anneke B., "Ivetta of Huy: Mater et Magistra." In *Sanctity and Motherhood: Essays on Holy Mothers in the Middle Ages*, edited by Anneke B. Mulder-Bakker, 225–58. New York: Garland, 1995.

_____, "Lame Margaret of Magdeburg: The Social Function of a Medieval Recluse." *Journal of Medieval History* 22 (1996): 155–69.

_____, *Lives of the Anchoresses: The Rise of the Urban Recluse in Medieval Europe*, translated by Myra Meerspink Scholz. Philadelphia: University of Pennsylvania Press, 2005.

Murk-Jansen, Saskia, *Brides in the Desert: The Spirituality of the Beguines*. Maryknoll, NY: Orbis Books, 1998.

_____, *The Measure of Mystic Thought: A Study of Hadewijch's Mengeldichten*. Göppingen, Germany: Kümmerle, 1991.

Neel, Carol, "The Origins of the Beguines." *Signs* 14:2 (Winter 1989): 322–41.

The New Dictionary of Catholic Spirituality, edited by Michael Downey. Collegeville, MN: The Liturgical Press, 1993.

New Trends in Feminine Spirituality: The Holy Women of Liège and Their Impact, edited by Juliette Dor, Lesley Johnson, and Jocelyn Wogan-Browne. Turnhout, Belgium: Brepols, 1999.

Newman, Barbara, *From Virile Woman to WomanChrist: Studies in Medieval Religion and Literature*. Philadelphia: University of Pennsylvania Press, 1995.

_____, "Possessed by the Spirit: Devout Women, Demoniacs, and the Apostolic Life in the Thirteenth Century." *Speculum* 73 (1998): 733–70.

Njus, Jesse, "The Politics of Mysticism: Elisabeth of Spalbeek in Context," *Church History*, 77 (2008): 285–317.

_____, *Vita Elizabeth sanctimonialis in Erkenrode*, private translation, 2007.

Nugent, Don Christopher, "The Harvest of Hadewijch: Brautmystik and Wesenmystik." *Mystics Quarterly* 12 (September 1986): 119–26.

Oliver, Judith, "Devotional Psalters and the Study of Beguine Spirituality." In *On Pilgrimage: The Best of Ten Years of Vox Benedictina*, edited by Margot King, 210–34. Toronto: Peregrina, 1994.

BIBLIOGRAPHY

_____, *Gothic Manuscript Illumination in the Diocese of Liege (c. 1250–c. 1330)*. Leuven: Uitgeverij Peeters, 1988.

_____, "'Je pecherise renc grasces a vos': Some French Devotional Texts in Beguine Psalters." In *Medieval Codicology, Iconography, Literature and Translation: Studies for Keith Val Sinclair*, edited by Peter Rolfe Monks and D. R. R. Owen, 248–62. Leiden: E. J. Brill, 1994.

Oort, Jessica van, "The Physical Actions of Medieval Women's Sacred Performances." *Magistra: A Journal of Women's Spirituality in History* 17:1 (Summer 2011): 3–30.

Ordained Women in the Early Church: A Documentary History, edited and translated by Kevin Madigan and Carolyn Osiek. Baltimore, MD: The Johns Hopkins University Press, 2005.

Osheim, Duane J., "Conversion, *Conversi*, and the Christian Life in Late Medieval Tuscany." *Speculum* 58 (1981): 368–90.

O'Sullivan, Robin, "The School of Love: Marguerite Porete's *Mirror of Simple Souls*." *Journal of Medieval History* 32 (2006): 143–62.

The Other Middle Ages: Witnesses at the Margins of Medieval Society, edited by Michael Goodrich. Philadelphia: University of Pennsylvania Press, 1998.

Panzer, Elizabeth Marie, *Cistercian Women and the Beguines: Interaction, Cooperation and Interdependence*. Ph.D., University of Wisconsin at Madison, 1994.

Papi, Anna Benvenuti, "Mendicant Friars and Female Pinzochere in Tuscany." Translated by Margery J. Schneider. In *Women and Religion in Medieval and Renaissance Italy*, edited by Daniel Bornstein and Roberto Rusconi, 84–103. Chicago: University of Chicago Press, 1996.

Pearson, J. Stephen, "St. Catherine of Genoa: Life in the Spiritual Borderlands." *Magistra: A Journal of Women's Spirituality in History* 12:2 (Winter 2006): 55–73.

Pedersen, Else Marie Wiberg, "Image of God–Image of Mary–Image of Woman: On the Theology and Spirituality of Beatrice of Nazareth." *Cistercian Studies Quarterly* 29:2 (1994): 209–20.

Pennings, Joyce, "Semi-religious Women in 15th Century Rome." *Mededelingen van het Nederlands Historisch Instituut te Rome* 12:47 (1987): 115–45.

Perry, Mary Elizabeth, *Gender and Disorder in Early Modern Seville*. Princeton, NJ: Princeton University Press, 1990.

Peterson, Ingrid J., *Clare of Assisi: A Biographical Study*. Quincy, IL: Franciscan Press, 1993.

Petroff, Elizabeth Alvilda, *Body and Soul: Essays on Medieval Women and Mysticism*. New York: Oxford University Press, 1994.

Phillips, Dayton, *Beguines in Medieval Strasburg: A Study of the Social Aspect of Beguine Life*. Palo Alto, CA: Stanford University Press, 1941.

Poor, Sara S., *Mechthild of Magdeburg and Her Book: Gender and the Making of Textual Authority*. Philadelphia: University of Pennsylvania Press, 2004.

Ranft, Patricia, *Women in Western Intellectual Culture, 600–1500*. New York: Palgrave, 2002.

Ray, Donna, "'There is a Threeness About You': Mechthild of Magdeburg's Theological Vision." *Magistra: A Journal of Women's Spirituality in History* 15:1 (Summer 2009): 77–103.

Revelations of Mechthild of Magdeburg, or The Flowing Light of the Godhead, translated by Lucy Menzies. London: Longmans, Green, 1953.

Rijpma, F. E., and G. J. R. Matt, *A Physical Anthropological Research of the Beguines of Breda 1267 to 1530 AD*. Leiden: Barge's Anthropologica, Leiden University Medical Center, 2005.

Rodgers, Susan, and Joanna E. Ziegler, "Elisabeth of Spalbeek's Trance Dance of Faith: A Performance Theory Interpretation from Anthropological and Art Historical Perspectives." In *Performance and Transformation: New Approaches to Late Medieval Spirituality*, edited by Mary A. Suydam and Joanna E. Ziegler, 299–355. New York: St. Martin's Press, 1999.

Rolfson, Helen, "Hadewijch, the List of the Perfect." *Vox Benedictina* 5 (1988): 277–87.

Ross, Ellen M., *The Grief of God: Images of the Suffering Jesus in Late Medieval England*. New York: Oxford University Press, 1997.

Rubin, Miri, *Corpus Christi: The Eucharist in Late Medieval Culture*. Cambridge, UK: Cambridge University Press, 1991.

Sandor, Monica, "Jacques de Vitry and the Spirituality of the *Mulieres Sanctae*." In *On Pilgrimage: The Best of Ten Years of Vox Benedictina*, edited by Margot King, 173–89. Toronto: Peregrina, 1994.

Send Me God: The Lives of Ida the Compassionate of Nivelles, Nun of la Ramée, Arnulf, Lay Brother of Villers, and Abundus, Monk of Villers, by Goswin of Bossut, translated and with an Introduction by Martinus Cawley, and with a Preface by Barbara Newman. University Park, PA: Pennsylvania State University Press, 2005.

Simons, Walter, "Architecture of Semi-Religiosity: The Beguinages of the Southern Low Countries, Thirteenth to Sixteenth Centuries." In *Shaping Community: The Art and Archeology of Monasticism. Papers from a Symposium Held at the Frederick R. Weisman Museum, University of Minnesota, March 10–12, 2000*, edited by Sheila McNally, 117–28. British Archaeological Reports International Series 941. Oxford, 2001.

———, "The Beguine Movement in the Southern Low Countries: A Reassessment." *Bulletin de l'Institut Historique Belge de Rome* 59 (1989): 63–105.

———, "Beguines and Psalters." *Oons geestelijk erf* 65 (1991): 23–30.

———, *Cities of Ladies: Beguine Communities in the Medieval Low Countries, 1200–1565*. Philadelphia: University of Pennsylvania Press, 2001.

———, "Reading a Saint's Body: Rapture and Bodily Movement in the *Vitae* of Thirteenth-Century Beguines." In *Framing Medieval Bodies*, edited by Sarah Kay and Miri Rubin, 10–23. Manchester: Manchester University Press, 1994.

———, "Staining the Speech of Things Divine: The Uses of Literacy in Medieval Beguine Communities." In *The Voice of Silence: Women's Literacy in a Men's Church*, edited by Therese de Hemptinne and Mara Eugenia Gongora, 85–110. Turnhout, Belgium: Brepols, 2004.

———, and J. E. Ziegler, "Phenomenal Religion in the Thirteenth Century and Its Image: Elisabeth of Spalbeek and the Passion Cult." *Women in the Church*, edited by

W. J. Sheils and Diana Wood. Studies in Church History 27, 117–26. Oxford: Basil Blackwell, 1990.

Sloan, Kathryn, *Women's Roles in Latin America and the Caribbean*. Westport, CT: Greenwood Publishing, 2011.

Snyder, Susan Renee Taylor, *Woman as Heretic: Gender and Lay Religion in Late Medieval Bologna*. Ph.D., University of California Santa Barbara, 2002.

Southern, R. W., *Western Society and the Church in the Middle Ages*. London: Penguin, 1970.

Stein, Frederick Marc, *The Religious Women of Cologne, 1120–1320*. Ph.D., Yale University, 1977.

Straeten, Katrien Vander, "A Study of Beatrice of Nazareth's *Van seuen manieren van heiliger minnen–Of seven manners of holy loving*." Accessed in March 2011 at http://cns. bu.edu/~satra/kaatvds/7mannersstudy.htm.

Suydam, Mary A., "Beguine Textuality: Sacred Performances." In *Performance and Transformation: New Approaches to Late Medieval Spirituality*, edited by Mary A. Suydam and Joanna E. Ziegler, 169–210. New York: St. Martin's Press, 1999.

_____, "Visionaries in the Public Eye: Beguine Literature as Performance." In *The Texture of Society: Medieval Women in the Southern Low Countries*, edited by Ellen E. Kittell and Mary A. Suydam, 131–52. New York: Palgrave Macmillan, 2004.

_____, "Women's Texts and Performances in the Medieval Southern Low Countries." In *Visualizing Medieval Performance: Perspectives, Histories, Contexts*, edited by Elina Gertsman, 143–59. Burlington, VT: Ashgate, 2008.

_____, "Writing Beguines: Ecstatic Performances." *Magistra: A Journal of Women's Spirituality in History* 2:1 (Summer 1996): 137–69.

Sweetman, Robert, "Christine of Saint-Trond's Preaching Apostolate: Thomas of Cantimpré's Hagiographical Method Revisited." *Vox Benedictina* (1992): 67–97.

_____, "Thomas of Cantimpré, *Mulieres Religiosae*, and Purgatorial Piety: Hagiographical Vitae and the Beguine 'Voice.'" In *A Distinct Voice: Medieval Studies in Honor of Leonard E. Boyle, OP*, edited by Jacqueline Brown and William P. Stoneman, 606–28. Notre Dame, IN: University of Notre Dame Press, 1997.

_____, "Thomas of Cantimpré: Performative Reading and Pastoral Care." In *Performance and Transformation: New Approaches to Late Medieval Spirituality*, edited by Mary A. Suydam and Joanna E. Ziegler, 133–67. New York: St. Martin's Press, 1999.

_____, "Visions of Purgatory and Their Role in the Bonum universale de apibus of Thomas of Cantimpré." *Ons Geestelijk Erf* 67 (1993): 20–33.

Tapia, Ralph, *The Alumbrados of Toledo: A Study in Sixteenth Century Spanish Spirituality*. Park Falls, WI: Weber and Sons, Inc., 1974.

Tar, Jane, "Angela of Foligno as a Model for Franciscan Women Mystics and Visionaries in Early Modern Spain." *Magistra: A Journal of Women's Spirituality in History* 11:1 (Summer 2005): 83–105.

Tarrant, J., "The Clementine Decrees on the Beguines: Conciliar and Papal Version." *Archivum historiae pontificiae* 12 (1974): 300–308.

Taylor, Judith Combes, *From Proselytizing to Social Reform: Three Generations of French Female Teaching Congregations, 1600–1720*. Ph.D., Arizona State University, 1980.

The Texture of Society: Medieval Women in the Southern Low Countries, edited by Ellen E. Kittell and Mary A. Suydam. New York: Palgrave Macmillan, 2004.

Thomas of Cantimpré: The Collected Saints' Lives: Abbot John of Cantimpré, Christina the Astonishing, Margaret of Ypres, and Lutgard of Aywières, edited and with an introduction by Barbara Newman. Translations by Margot H. King and Barbara Newman. Turnhout, Belgium: Brepols, 2008.

Thompson, Augustine, O.P., *Cities of God: The Religion of the Italian Communes 1125–1325*. University Park, PA: Pennsylvania State University Press, 2005.

Tobin, Frank, *Mechthild von Magdeburg: A Medieval Mystic in Modern Eyes*. Columbia, SC: Camden House, 1995.

Vandommele, Vincent, *The St.-Anna Hall of the St.-Elisabeth Beguinage in Kortrijk*. Master's thesis, R. Lemaire Centre for the Conservation of Historic Towns and Buildings, K.U. L. Leuven, 1996.

Van Eck, Xander, "Between Restraint and Excess: The Decoration of the Church of the Great Beguinage at Mechelen in the Seventeenth Century." *Simiolus: Netherlands Quarterly for the History of Art*, 28:3 (2000–2001): 129–62.

Van Engen, John, *Sisters and Brothers of the Common Life: The Devotio Moderna and the World of the Later Middle Ages*. Philadelphia: University of Pennsylvania Press, 2008.

The Voice of Silence: Women's Literacy in a Men's Church, edited by Therese de Hemptinne and Mara Eugenia Gongora. Turnhout, Belgium: Brepols, 2004.

Voices in Dialogue: Reading Women in the Middle Ages, edited by Linda Olson and Kathryn Kerby-Fulton. Notre Dame, IN: University of Notre Dame Press, 2005.

Walters, Barbara R., Vincent Corrigan, and Peter T. Ricketts, *The Feast of Corpus Christi*. University Park, PA: Pennsylvania State University Press, 2006.

Ward, Jennifer, *Women in Medieval Europe, 1200–1500*. London: Longmans, Green, 2002.

Warren, Nancy Bradley, *The Embodied Word: Female Spiritualities, Contested Orthodoxies, and English Religious Cultures, 1350–1700*. Notre Dame, IN: University of Notre Dame Press, 2010.

Waters, Claire, *Angels and Earthly Creatures: Preaching, Performance, and Gender in the Later Middle Ages*. Philadelphia: University of Pennsylvania Press, 2004.

Wiethaus, Ulrike, "The Death Song of Marie d'Oignies: Mystical Sound and Hagiographical Politics in Medieval Lorraine." In *The Texture of Society: Medieval Women in the Southern Low Countries*, edited by Ellen E. Kittell and Mary A. Suydam. New York: Palgrave Macmillan, 2004.

_____, "'For This I Ask You, Punish Me': Norms of Spiritual Orthopraxis in the Work of Maria van Hout (d. 1547)." *Ons Geestelijk Erf* 68:3 (1994): 253–70.

_____, *Maps of Flesh and Light: The Religious Experience of Medieval Women Mystics*. Syracuse, NY: Syracuse University Press, 1993.

_____, "Mechthild of Magdeburg." In *Christian Spirituality: The Classics*, edited by Arthur Holder. New York: Routledge, 2009.

_____, "Street Mysticism: An Introduction to 'The Life and Revelations of Agnes Blannbekin.'" In *Women Writing Latin from Roman Antiquity to Early Modern Europe, Vol. 2: Medieval Women Writing Latin*, edited by Laurie J. Churchill, Phyllis R. Brown, and Jan E. Jeffrey, 281–307. New York: Routledge, 2002.

Winston-Allen, Anne, *Convent Chronicles: Women Writing about Women and Reform in the Late Middle Ages*. University Park, PA: Pennsylvania State University Press, 2004.

Women in the Inquisition: Spain and the New World, edited by Mary E. Giles. Baltimore, MD: The Johns Hopkins University Press, 1999.

Women Preachers and Prophets through Two Millennia of Christianity, edited by Beverly Mayne Kienzle and Pamela J. Walker. Berkeley: University of California Press, 1998.

The Writings of Alijt Bake (1415–55): Mystic, Autobiographer, Prioress, Exile, translated by John Van Engen. Notre Dame, IN: University of Notre Dame Press, forthcoming.

Ziegler, Joanna E., "The Curtis Beguinages in the Southern Low Countries: Interpretation and Historiography." *Bulletin de l'Institut Historique Belge de Rome* 57 (1987): 31–70.

_____, "On the Artistic Nature of Elisabeth of Spalbeek's Ecstasy: The Southern Low Countries Do Matter." In *The Texture of Society: Medieval Women in the Southern Low Countries*, edited by Ellen E. Kittell and Mary A. Suydam, 181–202. New York: Palgrave Macmillan, 2004.

_____, "Reality as Imitation: The Role of Religious Imagery among the Beguines of the Low Countries." In *Maps of Flesh and Light: The Religious Experience of Medieval Women Mystics*, edited by Ulrike Wiethaus, 112–26. Syracuse, NY: Syracuse University Press, 1993.

_____, *Sculpture of Compassion: The Pietà and the Beguines in the Southern Low Countries, c. 1300–c. 1600*. Turnhout, Belgium: Brepols, 1992.

_____, "Secular Canonesses as Antecedent of the Beguines in the Low Countries: An Introduction to Some Older Views." *Studies in Medieval and Renaissance History* 13 (1992): 117–35.

_____, "Some Questions Regarding the Beguines and Devotional Art." In *On Pilgrimage: The Best of Ten Years of Vox Benedictina*, edited by Margot King, 463–76. Toronto: Peregrina, 1994.

Zum Brunn, Emilie, and Georgette Epiney-Burgard, *Women Mystics in Medieval Europe*. New York: Paragon House, 1989.

INDEX